THE CHURCH
AND
ITS MINISTRY

David Belgum, Ph.D.

PROFESSOR OF PASTORAL THEOLOGY
NORTHWESTERN LUTHERAN THEOLOGICAL SEMINARY

PRENTICE-HALL, INC.

Englewood Cliffs, N.J.

1963

*To my parents
who introduced me to
the Church and its Ministry
in our
parsonage home*

PRENTICE-HALL INTERNATIONAL, INC., *London*
PRENTICE-HALL OF AUSTRALIA, PTY., LTD., *Sydney*
PRENTICE-HALL FRANCE, S. A. R. L., *Paris*
PRENTICE-HALL OF JAPAN, INC., *Tokyo*
PRENTICE-HALL DE MEXICO, S.A., *Mexico City*
PRENTICE-HALL OF CANADA, LTD., *Toronto*

Library of Congress Catalog No.
63-10668

Printed in the United States of America
C-13364

TABLE OF CONTENTS

iii

PART I

THE CHURCH

INTRODUCTION

Criticism is heard from many quarters that the American churches are hyper-active. Overcrowded parish schedules, emphasis on "facilities," and too numerous projects are cited by those who believe theology is being minimized and that therefore the real mission of the church is being neglected. Yet *action* in and of itself is not an adequate criterion for criticism. One must ask whether the action is appropriate, necessary, timely, and founded upon solid theory and wholesome motivation.

We know that actions frequently make a greater impression and are remembered longer than words. If a clergyman teaches heretical doctrine, he will very likely be disciplined; but, if he violates the doctrine of the Church by his method of church administration, his administration of the Sacraments, or his use of pastoral care, the theological significance of his ministry is not so clearly seen. How we act can be just as significant as what we *say* we believe to be the total mission of the church.

Practical theology in the modern age attempts to explain the more theoretical branches of theology, such as systematic, biblical, and historical theology, to the parishioner in the local congregation who needs these truths and insights. Practical theology consists of those principles and methods needed to make the Gospel applicable to society and meaningful to the individual. This is much the same function as that performed by the production engineer in a modern factory, who stands in a functional relationship between the theoretician in the laboratory or at the drafting board, and the customer who will use the product. He is a vital link turning theory into practice. The old jibe at the ivory tower, "It's a wonderful theory, but it won't work," is simply not true. If it won't work, the theory is inadequate; and if it does work, there must be an explanation of it somewhere, even if it will never be learned in our lifetime. The task of practical theology is to keep theory and practice as closely related as possible.

The reason that there is a need for constant re-evaluation and re-adjustment in practical theology is that society, within which the church performs its mission, is constantly changing. This is nothing new for the Church, which has had to adjust serially to the age of the Roman Empire, the patterns of feudalism, absolute monarchy, the rise of an industrial and urban society, and finally to the nation-state forms of government in the modern age.

We shall divide our discussion into two parts. The first task is to understand what the Church is and why and how it expresses itself in certain tangible ways today. What is its unique mission and what factors must it take into account when trying to fulfill this mission in our world today? Secondly, we should consider the church's ministry to individuals in the crises of life by means of sacraments and rites. These are specific services rendered by the pastor on behalf of the Church. Although there are problems of consistency in the inclusion of specific services under Part Two, in contrast with the more general activities of the church as a whole under Part One (e.g., worship and preaching, Christian education and evangelism), the dividing principle has been to limit this latter section to services that are peculiarly tangible, specific, or personal.

Pastoral theology today is eager to benefit from the insights and research in the behavioral and social sciences. In many more places than the footnotes indicate, this book is indebted to concepts and theories of psychology, sociology, anthropology, psychiatry, and so forth, as they implement and supplement the understandings of the various theological departments. Such a cross-fertilization of disciplines is stimulating and useful. At the same time, it is precarious. Often, various schools of thought are based on quite contradictory basic assumptions, although on the surface, and for all practical purposes, they seem to be compatible. There is a great need for inter-disciplinary scholars to discover syntheses between the revelations of theology and the insights of the behavioral and social sciences. As specialization and the amount of knowledge increase, it will be even more important to encourage the dialogue between these two approaches to man and his problems. This is one task that the present study does not propose to accomplish, but it is hoped the reader will pick up hints and suggestions here and there that will be helpful.

In this discussion, theological definitions as expressed by various doctrinal systems are left for the reader to provide out of his own denominational tradition. When we discuss the concrete expressions of Christianity in the Church and the ministry, we speak from the advantage (or disadvantage) of a specific heritage and tradition. Nevertheless, it is hoped that the reader will sense in this discussion an ecumenical appreciation of the main currents of the Church's life through which the healing stream of the Gospel has flowed to minister to the needs of multitudes through the centuries.

The writer is indebted to a wide range of stimulating professors, parish pastors, and field work students, who have shared ideas and raised pertinent questions. Nothing is more helpful for a professor of practical theology than to be invited to speak to a group of parish clergy. In the discussion period, a diverse array of questions usually arise, prefaced by "What would you do in this situation?" or, "My experience has been exactly the opposite." Only by such contact with the living church is practical theology kept close to its real task. From the most unexpected sources have also come suggestions and implications for a better understanding of the role of the pastor toward his congregation. Perhaps most helpful have been the chance remarks of a personnel director, the long range planning of a hospital administrator, the experience of a social worker in defining her relationship with a client, the accuracy of an accountant or research scientist in handling statistics, and numerous others. The writer has a great debt to many who have stimulated or challenged him.

CHAPTER 1

ECCLESIA,

THE CALLED PEOPLE

The Greek word "ecclesia" was well chosen to describe the nature of the Church in New Testament times as well as to preserve the concept of the Chosen People in ancient Judaism. "Ecclesia" meant literally a group of people "called out" for a meeting or assembly. The Israelites believed that they had been chosen by God and that God had guided and directed their destiny. When God's people strayed away to idols and other gods, He called them back again. The whole contention of Scripture is that God took the initiative in gathering together a people who would later create a Church in his name.

In his explanation of the Third Article of the Apostles' Creed, Luther discusses the Church as follows, ". . . the Holy Ghost has called me by the Gospel . . . even as He calls, gathers, enlightens, and sanctifies the whole Christian Church on earth, and keeps it with Jesus Christ in the one true faith." The Church then is different in this regard from all other human associations. The origins of this group's existence are from God, and God is also the end of the group; that is, the Church exists to worship God and bring others to worship him in the "one true faith."

The New Testament Church began on the day of Pentecost when the Holy Spirit moved mightily through the preaching of the Gospel of the Risen Christ. In fact, the relationship between Christ and the Church was so close that the Church came to be thought of as the Mystical Body of Christ. Before the Incarnation, God had interjected Himself into the

7

historical experience of mankind only in the minds of those who sensed His presence. So Christ would remain in close fellowship with believers through a corporate incarnation, the social manifestation of his presence being the Mystical Body of Christ, or the Church. As Jesus had said, "Where two or three are gathered together in my name, there am I in the midst of them."

At the risk of over-extending this analogy of a social incarnation, it might be said that just as Christ's body became hungry, thirsty, tired, and felt pain upon the cross of Calvary, so the Church has had its physical and this-worldly manifestations. It too has been tired and weak, has suffered persecution, schism, and many of the experiences that are common to any social group. In our study it is these external manifestations that are the proper sphere of investigation. The acts of worship, ceremonies, organizational structure, institutions of mercy, Christian schools, church buildings, and so on might all be called the outward and tangible signs of an inward and spiritual grace (an expression describing the Sacraments). It is this type of expression that comes under the sphere of practical theology.

THE CHURCH AND CULTURE: SOCIOLOGICAL FACTORS

Inasmuch as Christianity expresses itself in the form of social institutions (among other ways), the Church in its various forms and activities is a suitable subject for sociological analysis. Yinger defines the sociology of religion as

> . . . the scientific study of the ways in which society, culture, and personality (or, in another sense, societies, cultures, and personalities), influence religion—influence its origin, its doctrines, its practices, the types of groups which express it, the kinds of leadership, etc. And, oppositely, it is the study of the ways in which religion affects society, culture, and personality—the processes of social conservation and social change, the structure of normative systems, the satisfaction or frustration of personality needs, etc. One must keep continuously in mind the interactive nature of these various elements.[1]

The interaction between culture and religious expression is quite obvious in Scripture. Many experiences of the Hebrew people would not be fully appreciated unless one considered their agrarian and nomadic culture. The same is true of Paul's various Epistles to churches under the Roman Empire.

---

[1] J. Milton Yinger, *Religion, Society and the Individual* (Part I), (New York: The Macmillan Company, 1957), pp. 20-21.

The Church influences and is influenced by social mores, ethnic loyalties and backgrounds, economic systems, political philosophies, and environmental conditions. The larger contrasts are most obvious. Consider the Norwegian Lutheran immigrants to the United States coming from the State Church of their homeland and dependent on itinerant pastors reaching their prairie settlements and sod huts. They counted heavily on a periodic and sacramental ministry. The Ohio frontier Methodists also relied on circuit rider preachers, but camp meetings and revivals, which were popular along the Ohio River Valley, would have been quite uncongenial to the stoical Norwegian Lutherans.

In mid-twentieth-century America, where a heterogeneous and mobile society is losing old loyalties and seeking security in new ones, clergymen are finding that church membership does not mean or imply what it used to. One study has suggested that a new problem for the church and the pastor is "the sociological basis of the theology of his parishioners. Whether Roman Catholic, Lutheran, or Congregationalist, a member of the upper-upper class or the lower-lower class shares the same basic theology as those of his class, regardless of denomination." [2] If this is true, it would be a rather startling example of the influence of culture upon the Church.

To the member of a quiet little country church with a hundred-year-old cemetery beside it, the modern church in one of our mushrooming suburbs will appear atrocious. Architecturally, the squat, rectangular "first unit" parish education "plant" will be unrecognized by the country cousin as being a church at all. One who considered the importance of doctrine to the Church would be startled by this suburban mission organizer's interpretation:

> I think this is the basic need—the need to belong to a group. You find this fellowship in a church better than anywhere else. And it is contagious. In a community like Park Forest, when young people see how many other people are going to church regularly, they feel they ought to. Another need is that of counseling. Young people want a place to take their problems and someone to talk to about them. Put all these things together and you get what we're after—a sense of community. We pick out the more useful parts of the doctrine to that end. [3]

One could ask why some denominations are more greatly influenced by their environment than others. Some, like the Mennonites, carry on with

---

[2] "An Appraisal of the 'Study of the Pastor's Week,'" Mimeographed, undated report of the Department of Theological Cooperation of the National Lutheran Council, page 3.

[3] William H. Whyte, Jr., *The Organization Man* (Garden City, New York: Doubleday and Company, Inc., 1956), pp. 406-07. (Copyright ©—1956 by William H. Whyte, Jr. By permission of Simon and Schuster, Inc.).

amazing disregard for society's demands or expectations. Still others insist on influencing the community by drastic and often therapeutic action.

Jesus had something to say about reform action: "You are the light of the world. A city set on a hill cannot be hid . . . Let your light so shine before men, that they may see your good works and give glory to your Father who is in heaven." [4] Also, the believers are to be "the salt of the earth" to preserve and benefit society; and, according to another figure of speech, they are to be the yeast that permeates the whole loaf. The ideal seems to point toward exerting a wholesome influence rather than being a passive object whom others influence as a "reed shaken in the wind."

Enthusiastic seminary graduates, filled with idealism, are likely to hope that such constructive action can suddenly take place with little or no consideration for the previous generations that have been influenced by society and have adapted to its culture and environment. It will call for heroic effort and revitalized spiritual motivation before many a stodgy old parish will answer the call to arms and march against some social, moral, or spiritual enemy in the community. A few pages taken from the notebooks of the sociology of religion will help a pastor harness his and the parish's energies to more realistic planning and action.

The wide divergence of attitudes within and between denominations on matters of marriage and divorce, entertainments and the arts, business, labor, property, slavery, government and political action, alcoholic beverages, censorship, stewardship, and "the Social Gospel," to say nothing of respective doctrines, is a long gamut indeed. Sociology of religion cannot and should not provide normative answers to the questions of schism. However, since many cleavages within the churches have had strong admixtures of social and cultural influences, and do not involve minimum essentials of the Christian witness, one can legitimately ask whether some of these conflicts could not have been avoided or at least resolved more constructively.

As Boisen so well documents the causes and "necessities" for the emergence of certain sects and splinter groups,[5] one is compelled to ask if somehow the Church could not have ministered to these people without their having to go elsewhere to find what they were looking for. Some feel out of place in the church because of their depressed economic condition; others seem to feel out of place temperamentally, be they at one extreme or the other of the introversion-extraversion scale. Social poise, educational-vocational level, and peculiar nationalistic or minority back-

---

[4] *Matthew* 5:14-16.

[5] Anton T. Boisen, *Religion in Crisis and Custom* (New York: Harper & Row, Publishers, 1955), Chapters 5 and 7.

ground can all be walls of separation. Saint Paul stated that, after Christ came to reconcile mankind to God and man to man, there need be no wall of separation between Jews and Greeks, nor between slave and freeman, nor between male and female.)

Perhaps one of the strengths of the Roman Catholic Church is that to support their tremendous spirit of worldwide uniformity there is almost no end of breaking down into small interest groups, thereby providing opportunities for almost anyone to feel he belongs and has some status. Here is an example of only one such specialized group: While many people might minimize the status and prestige of civil service employees, in one city a Saint Matthew's Guild, "an organization of Catholic employes of city and county . . . was established last year; when some 400 persons turned out for the first Communion breakfast." [6] They attend Mass in a body at a large downtown church and go directly to a fine hotel for the breakfast. One wonders if this does not mean a good deal to one who is "*just* a secretary for the city street department." The man in the tax office or men in numerous other occupations each have their saint with whom they can identify themselves. (One wonders what Protestant churches have done to encourage this feeling of identity, regardless of class or status, within the common fold. Frequently one sees persons transferring from one denomination to another as they are promoted on up the socio-economic ladder in their company or profession.)

A wider range of worship experiences, fellowship opportunities, educational approaches, and so forth might make it possible to unite a broader span of membership within the same church. Also a variety of projects for those not interested in or as capable in intellectual-social pursuits might give some persons a real sense of belonging which the present pace of competition does not allow. Some parishes have actually engaged a social worker specializing in group work to explore and analyze some of the sociological factors at work within the local church. These factors can be made to work for the aims of the church instead of against them. This brings us to another question, that of the inner dynamics of the church as a group.

THE COMMUNION OF SAINTS:
THE DYNAMICS OF GROUP MEMBERSHIP

Just as the term *ecclesia* indicates the relation of the Church to the world, the term *koinonia* characterizes the relationship of the members of the Church toward one another. The Church, viewed in-

[6] *The Minneapolis Star,* "Town Toppers," Friday, September 18, 1959, Section A, p. 9.

ternally in the words of the Apostles' Creed, is "the Communion of Saints." One must enter the interior life of the believer to discover the significance of his membership in a church. This implies a subjective point of view which an outsider may never fully achieve, but can only approximate by observation, discussion, and inference. We now have tools for studying the dynamics of group interaction and the significance of group membership. They can be a great help to the pastor in his work as a leader of church groups as well as a help to the whole congregation.

In one sense, of course, the focus of Christianity is upon God, who is uncaused, omnipotent, and has no *needs* in the sense in which we think of the human needs of hunger, thirst, sex, recognition, security, and group support. In another sense, the church has another focus and that is upon the needs of mankind. Man is finite and has many needs which must be satisfied or he cannot bear this existence. Yinger, in a broad definition of religion, shows this relationship between man's finitude, his personal and social needs, and the nature of religion.

> The human individual, blessed (and sometimes cursed) with the power of language, capable, therefore, of anticipating the future, including a foreknowledge of his own death, able to verbalize ideal states, to create standards, is continually threatened with failure, with frustration, with his conception of justice unfulfilled. These problems tend to loom up as overwhelming or "absolute evils." Religion is man's attempt to "relativize" them by interpreting them as part of some larger good, some conception of the absolute that puts the individual's problems into new perspective, thus to remove or reduce their crushing impact . . . there is (also) the tendency of each individual to think only of himself, to make his joys, his desires into "absolute goods," threatening the patterns of mutual adjustment that social life requires. Religion is the attempt to "relativize" the individual's desires, as well as his fears, by subordinating them to a conception of absolute goods more in harmony with the shared and often mutually contradictory needs and desires of human groups.[7]

Christianity assumes that these needs of man are met within the fellowship of believers. A few mystics and hermits have felt little or no need for the social intercourse, but this is hardly the intention of Jesus nor the general experience of the Church. Believers are like stones in the temple, "fitly joined together" with Christ as the cornerstone. The relations are so close that Christ referred to himself as the vine and to believers as the branches growing together as a living organism. Another metaphor to show mutual interdependence is that of the foot that cannot do without the hand, both of which are useless without the head. Thus, any discussion in practical theology concerning the nature of the Church must take full cognizance of its social relations.

[7] *Op. cit.*, pp. 15-16.

Students of group dynamics have discovered that, among other things, a group's energy is largely used to fulfill two functions: moving toward an agreed upon goal ("group locomotion") and maintaining the group as such ("group cohesiveness").[8] For the church, the *goal* is the redemption of the individual and the reconciliation of a hostile society to God. The church must also direct considerable effort toward the maintenance of "cohesiveness." Jesus' parables about the Kingdom of Heaven indicate charateristics of this fellowship. Consider the parables of the wheat and the weeds, the sheep and the goats, the good tree bearing good fruit and the corrupt tree destined to be cast into the fire. In short, it is quite possible to divide those who are inside the group from those who are outside, those who belong to the Kingdom from those who belong to the world.

The very concept "group" implies membership; there must be standards, admission procedures, marks of identity to show participation with other members of the group, and finally, ways of withdrawing or being excluded from the group. Although this has been true of primitive tribes and more elaborate human associations for a long time, the implications for many Christian churches have not been seen by ministers and official parish boards. Some have thought it unChristian and *undemocratic* to be too strict about the standards for admission to church membership. An even more touchy problem is to contemplate dropping someone "from the roll." Yet the significance and importance of church membership no doubt varies in the minds of the members in direct ratio to the standards and expectations of the group as a whole, including its leaders.

One has only to compare the attitude toward excommunication from the Roman Catholic Church and the possibility of being "dropped" from one of the more democratic and less tightly knit Protestant churches to draw some interesting inferences concerning the significance of membership in the respective groups. Although the author has not made a systematic study of it (and it would be a most suitable subject for thorough research), casual observation has led him to believe that the "lapsed members list" is not quite as long where adequate instruction and preparation for church membership is carried out. Sometimes only a brief "orientation to the plant facilities, schedule, and activities" is all that is involved. This casual attitude toward membership in the church plus little follow-up and integration into the fellowship of the group usually corresponds with little loyalty and less sacrifice for the goals of the church. What a contrast to the standards laid down by the Synod of Elvira in the year 305 A.D., which required a two-year program of inquiry, private and class

---

[8] See Part Two and Part Four of *Group Dynamics: Research and Theory,* edited by Dorwin Cartwright and Alvin Zander (Evanston, Illinois: Row, Peterson and Company, 1953), especially Chapters 7 and 22.

instruction, attendance at the Mass as "hearers," and final preparation for Baptism.[9] The need for church members was hardly less in that day, and, note, it was initiated before Constantine gave the Church official sanction.

Since groups minister to the diverse needs of many individuals, it is natural that the various members should sometimes desire to stress their own individual needs, problems, and special interests. The most zealous and individualistic members sometimes find it hard to discipline themselves and focus their attention on the group goal, the task or objective agreed upon by the majority. Considering the rich array of doctrines and the variety of ministries involved in the total Church, no wonder schism has been a continuing problem. Even in the local congregation one feels that sanctification should be stressed more; another reserves judgment on sin; still another emphasizes the Atonement. Each has his own hierarchy and priority of doctrines and practices, those which he feels to be essential and those which are non-essential. One mounts his political hobby horse and emphasizes the importance of foreign missions; another advocates charity work in orphanages; another feels Bible study groups are the life blood of the church; still another sees sobriety and temperance as the most important mission of the church.

In one sense, a variety of emphases is a good thing, and most groups allow for and even encourage such diversity. The Church Year deliberately stresses various doctrines in sequence so that none of the facets of Christianity will be overlooked. Thus, Christmas reminds us of the Incarnation, Holy Week of the Atonement, and Pentecost of the work of the Holy Spirit. Most denominations follows a "calendar of causes" stressing Christian education one month, works of mercy another month, foreign missions and world relief at another time, and so forth. However, if one or another aspect is over-emphasized or neglected, "subgroups" form in an effort to counterbalance whatever such persons feel is being misrepresented. This beginning of cleavage, clique, or schism may or may not be "justifiable" or "reasonable"; the important thing to consider is that it makes excellent sense to those who are involved. To complicate matters, both reasonable and neurotic motivations, constructive and destructive forces, are sometimes at work among a motley assortment who advocate a new "movement."

---

[9] See Lewis J. Sherrill's excellent book *The Rise of Christian Education* (New York: The Macmillan Company, 1944), which traces this subject from early Hebrew beginnings to modern times. There are many interesting references to the symbols, ceremonies, and significance of religious membership both Jewish and Christian.

See also Joseph E. McCabe, *The Power of God in a Parish Program* (Philadelphia: The Westminster Press, 1959), Chapter 4, "Receiving Members." The author presents his experiment with raising standards for church membership and shows the favorable reception of it by the members and its good results.

When new members come into a group, there is a period in which the group exudes a sense of tension until it knows whether the new members will disrupt the group. When one member moves too fast and too far, causing potential splits in the group, a quiet resistant movement grows within the group.

A group is fearful of conflict when the conflict promises to destroy the group. . . . The difference lies in whether the conflict threatens the basic group being. Warfare is tolerated—is even fun—until it threatens the basic survival of the group.[10]

One of the difficulties in the Church has been the fact that clergy and lay leaders have taken for granted that differences and conflicts are essentially theological and are to be resolved primarily on an intellectual basis. This is indeed an important part of the picture. The realistic Church historian, however, sees the problem of congregational fights and split parishes (as well as broken denominations and splinter sects) as a much more complex problem, fraught with social and personal implications and breakdowns in the group process and interpersonal relationships.

We have given only a general consideration to some of the practical aspects of the Church and its nature as a social institution related to the Kingdom of God, to the culture in which it finds itself, and to the needs of its members. The specific expressions of these questions in the local parish, and some proposed approaches to solutions of these problems, will be dealt with in more detail in later chapters of this section.

Our focus of attention will not be the invisible Church, but the tangible Church as we encounter it as a social institution in mid-twentieth-century America. Even though the Holy Spirit builds the Church as such, all that is available for our investigation is the human manifestation of the churches: their buildings and activities, their ceremonies and organizational structures, their stated goals and their actual practices.

[10] From an article "Some Forces That Operate below the Surface" by Leland Bradford in *Encyclopedia for Church Group Leaders*, edited by Lee J. Gable (New York: Association Press, 1959), pp. 239-40. The entire Chapter 7, "What is Important about Group Process" (composed of six articles), provides an excellent discussion of the emphasis, which is hinted at, but beyond the scope of the present volume.

CHAPTER 2

WORSHIP
AND THE CHURCH'S
UNIQUE MINISTRY

The central mission of the Church is the worship of God and the proclamation of the Gospel. Christianity has relinquished various other tasks, such as works of mercy and education, which at one time it considered its own obvious duty, to other agencies of society. There was a time when practically all hospitals and schools were operated by the Church. However, the churches have never thought that any other agency could take its place in directing the hearts of people to God in worship nor in preaching the Word of God, which is almost always a major function in the worship services of the Church.

Quite different factors have at times tempted the churches to put worship on a par with other activities. The Enlightenment on the one hand, and the Social Gospel on the other, tended to de-emphasize worship as the central purpose of the Church. Today, one often senses this lack of priority as one reads the Sunday morning bulletin announcing next Sunday morning's worship services, and in the same breath, announcing activities of the Boy Scouts, the choir practice, the Tabitha Guild, the Sunday School Teachers' Meeting, and the Men's Brotherhood. These are all "activities" that are available to members. Sometimes, how many were "gotten out" for the Fathers and Sons Banquet is considered just as good a gauge of the "success" of the church as how many were "gotten out" for a worship service. This ought to be vigorously counteracted by careful re-interpretation of the mission of the church.

When Dr. Carl E. Lund-Quist was a pastor at the University of Minnesota, responsible for thousands of students, he stated that he was not concerned about any of his students who did not attend the wide variety of social and discussion type activities at the student center if he were assured that such students were in church for worship Sunday mornings and regularly receiving Communion. If worship of God is kept central in a believer's life, the rest will take care of itself.

It is discouraging to see many a young mission congregation building their "first unit," only to discover that worship is being relegated to the level of an adaptation. "We can adapt this fellowship hall, which is used so much during the week, for our Sunday morning worship services by pulling back these drapes and moving the furniture about," explained one member of a mission. It was not just a chance remark, for the more one explored the significance of worship in the life of this new congregation, the less important it appeared in light of many other demands upon the facilities and the schedule. Even on the one hour reserved for worship, it was considerably adapted to "fit in with the Sunday School schedule."

This is hardly the Old Testament's interpretation of the centrality of worship, nor does it reflect the post-Pentecost Church, which particularly thrived on the gathering together, if need be in catacombs, to be fed on the Bread of Life and to sing hymns of praise. A re-reading of the twentieth chapter of *Exodus* impresses one with the priority and centrality of the worship of and relationship to God. We need to consider the variety of ways this can be carried out in our churches.

THE FUNCTION OF LITURGY
AND SYMBOLISM

Liturgical practices have been discussed and judged for many strange purposes. They have been controversial battle flags used to designate rival factions and denominational distinctiveness, to mark off "high church" from "low church" tendencies, and to characterize the development of church life and varying emphases in doctrine.

Although the disciplines of anthropology and social psychology have been paying increasing attention to rites of passage and ritualistic behavior, not enough attention has been given to the study of liturgy as such from an objective point of view. What does liturgy do to meet the various needs of the individuals participating in it? This question is not meant to imply that some pragmatic psychological test can determine for the Church the validity of its traditions or the legitimacy of its forms of worship. Yet to understand more fully the dynamics and psychological significance of liturgy can help us to participate in this experience more meaningfully.

Definitions

Liturgy is a term derived from the Greek word λειτουργία originally meaning "at Athens, and elsewhere . . . *public service* performed by private citizens at their own expense . . . , *public service* of the gods . . . , *the service* or *ministry* of priests LXX." [1] This is referred to in *Numbers* 8:24-26 as the function of the Levites.

There is some question as to whether New Testament usage stressed the priestly character of this service or whether it was to be shared by all the believers. But this discussion is aside from the purpose of the present investigation. The point is that it has come to have a specific meaning in our time. For the purposes of this study the term is intended in the broad sense and not in the narrow sense of "The Liturgy," referring only to the Eucharist.

> The Evangelical confessions gave preference to the term *caerimonia;* and it was only under the influence of Humanism, beginning with the sixteenth century, that the word *liturgia* came into current use, first among the Roman Catholics, and later among the Protestants. The term is now often applied in a widened sense, and the phrases baptismal, marriage, confirmation, and burial liturgies are loosely employed.[2]

Our discussion here does not concern itself with questions of the best or most correct forms, but rather with the significance of the fact that such forms are prescribed *per se.*

Relation Between Liturgical and Mystical Experiences

Mystical experiences seem to be available to or achieved by a very few persons in the history of the Church. In Biblical times, the experiences of Moses, Isaiah, Saint Paul, and Saint Stephen come to mind. Seemingly, as William James described mystical experiences, the senses are not much involved; nor are concrete terms, tangible imagery, or deliberate action. The mystic usually experiences the impact of the religious encounter in isolation and not within the context of social relationships—note how many mystics were hermits or were alone at the

---

[1] Henry George Liddell and Robert Scott, *A Greek-English Lexicon* (revised edition), Volume II. (London: Oxford University Press, 1940), p. 1036.

See also A Catholic Dictionary, by William E. Addis and Thomas Arnold (16th edition, revised), (London: Routledge & Kegan Paul Limited, 1957), page 514. "The theocratic constitution of the Jewish commonwealth naturally led the Septuagint translators to use λειτουργία and the kindred forms chiefly of the services of God in the sanctuary."

[2] Samuel Macauley Jackson (editor-in-chief), *The New Schaff-Herzog Encyclopedia of Religious Knowledge,* Volume VI. (Grand Rapids, Michigan: Baker Book House, 1950), p. 499.

time of their experience. Sometimes they were away from home on a pilgrimage.

Persons who have not had unique mystical experiences should not deny that there is real value therein for people so blessed. However, the mystical experience, usually devoid of props, patterns, guides, and sensory aids, can not be planned for and scheduled as a part of Church life, since to do so usually creates spurious and synthetic imitations of true mysticism.

Let us not try to limit God to either the mystical or the liturgical mode of communicating with us, but be open and available for as many ways possible whereby we might receive the Lord's blessings. Much breath and energy has been wasted on insisting that everyone must meet God in like fashion. Moses met God in the burning bush of the open country, and Isaiah met Him in the sanctuary, through the firing coals on the altar. Allport shows us why most persons need ritual aids.

> For the great majority of people the solitariness of the religious quest becomes a burden. . . . The expressive symbols of ritual aid the individual by eliciting intentions that would otherwise lie mostly dormant. In psychological parlance, ritual is a form of social facilitation which intensifies the comparable attitudes and sentiments of all participants.[3]

Precisely because there are relatively few truly spontaneous persons, the Church has found it helpful to provide a variety of aids for worship, among them rites and ceremonies, liturgical practices and symbolic forms. To understand these aids more fully we must examine the process of symbolization.

The Function and Power of Symbolism

The term "symbol" comes from the Greek συμ and βάλλειν, and means simply to throw together. Thus one can bring together or associate an abstract idea, past experience, or event with a concrete object. If this is done repeatedly, a symbol evolves. Yet this is not so much a deliberate action as it is the natural consequence or by-product of basically meaningful experience, commonly perceived and shared. Ernst Cassirer, in his comprehensive work, *The Philosophy of Symbolic Forms*, has made a thorough analysis of the phenomena of symbolization:

> In it (the concept of the symbol) we have attempted to encompass the totality of those phenomena in which the sensuous is in any way filled with meaning, in which a sensuous content, while preserving the mode of its existence and facticity, represents a particularization and embodi-

[3] Gordon W. Allport, *The Individual and His Religion* (New York: The Macmillan Company, 1953), p. 135.

ment, a manifestation and incarnation of a meaning. . . . However deeply we may penetrate into the formations of the sensuous, spiritual consciousness, we never find this consciousness absolutely objectless, as something absolutely simple, prior to all separations and distinctions.[4]

In short, symbolization must necessarily take place in some degree. As Cassirer says in his first volume on *Language*:

True, *human* knowledge can nowhere dispense with symbols and signs; but it is precisely this that characterizes it as human, i.e., limited and finite in contradistinction to the ideal of the perfect, archetypal and divine intellect.[5]

There does seem to be a universal need for symbolization. We find widespread use of symbolic forms and language in widely scattered and sometimes most unexpected spheres of life. Chemists and mathematicians use intricate symbols and formulae to represent physical elements, quantities, and relationships, which are completely unintelligible to any but the initiated, scientific priesthood. The policeman not only *is* more authoritative, he *feels* and *acts* with greater authority and confidence when he is wearing his badge, special headgear, and is carrying a night stick by his side. Many a bad little boy has not had to be clubbed senseless to change his mind about stealing candy from the shop counter; the mere sight of the policeman's badge and uniform is equivalent to strong words and actions. The judge symbolizes his impartiality and justice by clothing himself in judicial robes (and, if British, a long, white wig) and makes his pronouncements from "the bench" in a room whose whole setting and agenda speak for "the people" of the community or nation.

Erwin Goodenough has this to say about the power of symbols in his comprehensive study of Jewish symbols:

In general, a symbol is a word or form which expresses more than it indicates, and so has power beyond its literal denotation. The religious symbol is not only a direct purveyor of meaning in itself, but also a thing of power, or value, operating upon us to inspire, to release tensions, to arouse guilt, or to bring a sense of forgiveness and reconciliation. We may love the symbol, we may hate it, but so long as it is a symbol we register its message, feel its power.[6]

---

[4] Ernst Cassirer, *The Philosophy of Symbolic Forms,* Volume III: *The Phenomenology of Knowledge* (Translated by Ralph Manheim), (New Haven, Connecticut: Yale University Press, 1957), p. 93.

[5] Ernst Cassirer, *The Philosophy of Symbolic Forms,* Volume I: *Language* (Translated by Ralph Manheim), (New Haven, Connecticut: Yale University Press, 1953), p. 112.

[6] Erwin R. Goodenough, *Jewish Symbols in the Greco-Roman Period,* Volume IV: *The Problem of Method, Symbols from Jewish Cult* (New York: Pantheon Books (Bollingen Foundation), 1954), p. 33.

No wonder that Christianity, which aims to touch man at the heights and depths of his being, should utilize symbolic forms, words, and actions.

There appears to be a direct correlation between the seriousness or depth of human emotion involved and the amount of symbolization deemed necessary. Thus, in the death struggle of military organizations preparing for war, there is no end of parading, firing of salutes, inspection of ranks, changes of posture, hoisting of flags, careful delineation of class, status, and power, exhibition of battle ribbons, appropriate formalized greeting in the form of saluting, standing in exact spatial relationships to one another, and so forth. Without these symbols to support and implement social control, it is doubtful whether a million men would, at a given signal, voluntarily, spontaneously, and simultaneously go against the basic drives of self-preservation and the preservation of the race. Thus powerful are symbols in the life of man.

It is possible that some aspects of our existence are so powerful and meaningful that thoughts and words are generally inadequate channels of expression when we wish to communicate with our fellows. Fromm hints at this continuum and gradation stressing the action aspect of ritual.

> Just as the symbolic language which we find in dreams and in myths is a particular form of expressing thoughts and feelings by images of sensory experience, the ritual is a symbolic expression of thoughts and feelings by *action*.[7]

It is no wonder that worship must include action as well as thought and word.[8] Consider the powerful instinct of hunger and the accompanying rituals of toasting honored guests, proper use of a great variety of silverware, courtesies and amenities. One might ask if all this is really necessary for the nutrition of the body and to satisfy the instinct of hunger. No doubt exactly because "the breaking of bread" is so basically essential to our existence, it became a suitable vehicle for deep spiritual symbolism from earliest Old Testament times.

One could also consider the sexual instinct and the complex development of ceremonies and rituals involved in marriage and family life. It would be an interesting study in itself to trace out whether there is any correlation between the weakening of the modern family and the increasing lack of traditional, customary, and symbolic activity within the family circle—inattention to the family altar, oversight of anniversaries, simplification and secularization of the celebration of Christmas, birthdays, and so forth within the family.

---

[7] Erich Fromm, *Psychoanalysis and Religion* (New Haven, Connecticut: Yale University Press, 1950), p. 109.

[8] *Cf.*, Evelyn Underhill, *Worship*, Chapter 2, "Ritual and Symbol" (New York: Harper and Brothers, 1936), (First Harper Torchbook Edition published 1957).

If the above hypothesis concerning the symbolization and the meaningfulness of human experience is correct, then we would not be surprised to find varied and intensive use of symbols in religious experience. Consider the widespread use and elaboration of the theme of the cross and crucifix. Tyrrell has said, "The crucifix is the collective sin of the world made visible." [9] Mere words and intellectual concepts cannot adequately express the sin, failure, and tragedy of the world of men.

Carl Gustav Jung has made the greatest contribution in showing the really deep levels from which symbols may arise and to whom they may be addressed.[10] With his concept of the "collective unconscious," he suggests not only that it is necessary to come to grips with issues in our unconscious reservoir of personal experience, but we must become reconciled to our heritage. As Isaiah wrote, "Look to the rock from which you were hewn, and to the quarry from which you were digged." [11] Symbols become the language that communicates not only from person to person but from generation to generation. Therefore, the children of Israel left a symbolic pile of stones on the west bank of the River Jordan so that future generations might ask questions about their past. ". . . that this may be a sign among you, when your children ask in time to come, 'What do these stones mean to you?'" [12] The same Jehovah who was caring for them had been concerned about their fathers.

Jung stresses the need of modern man to re-experience the "collective unconscious," to accept and share with his ancestors the great issues of life. Modern man underestimates the value of the religious and social experiences of his predecessors with a haughty confidence that he has earned sophisticated independence in his own generation. Jung contends that man should not try to leap over the stages of development which undergird his present culture, but should rather seek to incorporate them in his present existential experience. This calls for a humility born out of respect and appreciation for the past and its contributions. Zoologists claim that ontogeny recapitulates phylogeny. The history of the individual tends to repeat the history of the race. For an individual to neglect or reject his religio-cultural past or his collective unconscious would be as unrealistic as trying to skip from infancy to adulthood by omitting childhood and adolescence, which some unfortunate people have been forced to do with tragic consequences to their final maturity.

Grensted discusses the development of religion both in the individual

[9] George Tyrrell, *External Religion* (London: Longmans, Green & Co., 1906).

[10] Carl Gustav Jung, *Modern Man in Search of a Soul* (Translated by W. S. Dell and C. F. Baynes), (New York: Harcourt, Brace and Company, 1933).

See also *Psychology and Religion* (New Haven, Connecticut: Yale University Press, 1950).

[11] *Isaiah* 51:1b.

[12] *Joshua* 4:6.

and the race and makes similar mention of the relationship between symbolism and the unconscious:

> It seems to be clear that this process of adjustment to life and its various situations and problems by dramatic symbol and action rather than by reasoning is characteristic of every level of the unconscious psyche, so far as we can read it and its ways. It only reaches expression at the conscious level by making alliance with related symbols, which thus may carry latent meanings of unexpected depth and force. There is a hint here of an answer to the well-known philosophical problem of the relation between verbal symbol, or idea, and meaning, which may perhaps best be approached from the side of affect and conation, rather than from that of rational concept.[13]

We need to apply these generalizations to the concrete situation of pastoral care to see its implication for religious experience.

The power of symbols to evoke emotions and ideas is well known to every pastor who has ministered to a semiconscious patient lying motionless and apparently unreachable for days, and whose lips move or eyelids flicker at the confession of the Creed, the praying of the Lord's Prayer, or the pronouncement of the Benediction. Jung found that many of his very ill patients, who could not speak or think logically, would communicate through the ancient symbols of fire, water, wind, the square, the circle, blood, and other basic elements of human existence that represent primitive experiences.

It should not seem strange to anyone familiar with the variety of ways in which God worked with and through the people of the Bible, that the Holy Spirit should call and strengthen and minister to people's needs through the unconscious level of the personality as well as through the conscious level. In fact, Saint Paul suggests as much in his *Letter to the Romans* (8:26): "Likewise the Spirit helps us in our weakness; for we do not know how to pray as we ought, but the Spirit himself intercedes for us with sighs too deep for words." In saying this, Paul does not suggest any peculiar pan-psychism, or equating the Spirit with the unconscious, conscious, or any other one part of the human personality. Rather, we may envision God dealing with man through that aspect by which He can help us most effectively.

Liturgical practices utilize the folded hands and outstretched arms, the sign of the cross, the procession and bended knee, confession, absolution, benediction, and other traditional customs that have evolved out of the experience of our ancestors and represent values and forces that are as efficacious for our lives as they were for our fathers' and our fathers' fathers. Thus liturgy conserves the gains of the past. Yet it is dynamic,

[13] L. W. Grensted, *The Psychology of Religion* (New York: Oxford University Press, 1952), pp. 105-06.

and has continued to absorb and incorporate the unique experiences and spiritual struggles of each ensuing generation. In fact, this is the unique value of liturgy: that it can conserve and grow in dynamic interaction. Even to this day there is revision of liturgical forms while the basic elements and intentions are preserved.

Security

The constant craving of man for security, and his relentless struggle to find it, may date back to the first primitive who discovered he would be safer from wild animals if a large bonfire could be kept blazing. How relieved we are when it is apparent someone or something can be depended upon, whether it be a high bridge, an accurate alarm clock, the weekly paycheck, one's parents or friends, one's employer or spouse, or some routine of daily life!

The writer recalls the fascination with which he watched commuters board the homebound streetcar in the center of the city when he was a conductor on the lines. It became apparent that an amazing rhythm of regularity held these milling masses in its grip. There was an astounding consistency with which the same faces would appear on the 4:35 or the 5:56 car. After a hard day battling in the marketplace, some even stood until their favorite seat was vacated, even though many other places were unoccupied.

Why this great value placed upon regularity, security of habit, and the familiar? It is not unrelated to the preceding section on the unconscious. Freud alerted us to the fact that man may have as much to fear from his unconscious drives and hidden conflicts as from the dangers of the outer world. But consider the uncertainties of man's modern situation; the danger of war, his social and geographic mobility, his dependence upon a wavering stock market, the climatic changes of drought and flood, hurricane and fire, and the ever-present possibility of death to himself or his loved ones, disease and accident, confounded by his own fickle temperament. It is little wonder that man prizes security and turns to God as a refuge and strength, that he desires to be safe in the Everlasting Arms.

The regularity and dependability of the liturgy with its familiar forms, its reliable invocation of the Creator of all things, its unwavering absolution and repeated assurance of salvation, its certain benediction can all be counted on regardless of the changes and vicissitudes of man's encounter with the weather, fluctuating fortunes in his vocation, and the moods and whims which cause him inner insecurity. The Church through the centuries, and the children of Israel for centuries before that, patterned liturgical forms of worship to meet this basic need of mankind for security. They are forms that truly represent the unchangeable God and the Christ who is the same yesterday, today, and forever.

Liturgical forms serve as supportive and controlling forces when the threats and pressures of life become too great, either from the outer world or from our inner unconscious drives. Control is needed amidst great crises. This is why liturgies have been developed not only around the celebration of Holy Communion but also around the sacrament of Baptism, the Confirmation of the adolescent, Marriage, and Burial. In a symposium entitled *Sociological Theory*, there is a discussion that is pertinent at this point. William Thomas is quoted as follows:

> Control is the end to be secured and attention is the means of securing it. They are the objective and subjective sides of the same process. Attention is the mental attitude which takes note of the outside world and manipulates it; it is the organ of accommodation. But attention does not operate alone; it is associated with habit on the one hand and with crisis on the other. . . . The incidents of birth, death, adolescence, and marriage, while not unanticipated, are, always foci of attention and occasions for control.[14]

If it has been shown that, psychologically, liturgy is designed to minister to man's insecurity by providing a dependable frame of reference within which he can draw upon the great power of religious experience, the next task should be to describe more in detail the nature of this framework, these forms.

Educational Reinforcement and Participation

Modern psychology of learning teaches that the fullest possible involvement of the whole personality is necessary to achieve the maximum results in education. An idea or concept or belief will be more firmly imbedded in the memory and will more likely influence behavior if it has been reinforced by emotional overtones and appropriate action. Evelyn Underhill indicates how ritual undergirds man's religious experience and involves all his faculties:

> Ritual weaves speech, gesture, rhythm and agreed ceremonial into the worshipping action of man; and thus at its best can unite his physical, mental, and emotional being in a single response to the Unseen. The use of symbols and images—which is, in some form or degree, a feature of

---

[14] William I. Thomas, *Source Book for Social Origins* (Chicago: The University of Chicago Press, 1909), pp. 16-17.

(See other articles from a variety of disciplines related to the subject of social controls in *Sociological Theory*, edited by Edgar F. Borgatta and Henry J. Meyer, New York: Alfred A. Knopf, 1956.)

every cultus—is again forced on him by his own psychological peculiari-
ties; the fact that all his thinking and feeling is intimately related to that
world of things in which he lives.[15]

Is not the heresy of rationalism that it was aware of only part of man's
nature and glorified the cerebrum at the expense of other useful and
necessary parts. Contrariwise, perhaps the error of pietist extremists is
their over-emphasis of emotion and the equally unfortunate neglect of
other aspects of man's nature. Such segmented views of man are characteristic of philosophical and theological fads. There remains the con-
tiuing need to recognize that God created *all* of man, cerebrum, endocrine
glands, sense perception, and so forth. Theology must be eclectic to
avoid taking a narrow view of God's relationship to human existence.

Besides imitation of the action of others, repetition is a strong ally of
the learning process. There is a direct correlation between repetition and
retention within the memory. But repetition does more than reinforce
factual learning; it also creates and tends to perpetuate a certain mental
set or attitude so that the individual is inclined to grow in loyalty toward
certain goals and values as he repeatedly acts in accordance with those
goals. Thus in Christian worship, repeated prayer and acts of devotion
tend to help the believer view all of life in an attitude of prayer and
faith, and with a devout sense of stewardship toward, and worship of, the
God who created him.

Liturgy allows full participation of the whole person through all of the
five senses. Thus the sense of sight takes in the message of the stained
glass windows and the behavior of the pastor and other believers in the
church; [16] the sense of hearing receives the verbal messages, the hymns,
and worshipful responses; the sense of taste receives the bread and wine
of the Holy Communion; the sense of touch is activated in various pos-
tures while kneeling or folding the hands; and in some instances, the
aroma of the wine or the smell of incense create sensations that remain
permanently associated with worship. It is a well-accepted fact that modes
of action have outlived modes of thinking or feeling. The action of battle
leaves a far greater impression on the soldier than the intellectual information of his basic training instruction manual.

Today, there is a new appreciation of the advisability and appropriate-

[15] Evelyn Underhill, *Worship* (New York: Harper and Row, Inc., 1936, Torchbook
Edition, 1957), p. 37.

[16] Jurgen Ruesch, a psychiatrist, and Weldon Kees, a photographic artist, have
made a fascinating study of the nonverbal process of communicating ideas, emotional
states, values, and social relationships through objects, posture, movements, and visu-
ally perceived relationships. Such symbolic communication may suffice in and of itself
or it may support and intensify verbal and rational language. See their *Nonverbal
Communication, Notes on the Visual Perception of Human Relations* (Berkeley, California: University of California Press, 1956).

ness of opening the whole self to God's message and responding to God's grace with mind, feelings, and action. Consider how Jesus' classic summation of the Ten Commandments admonishes us to love God with our whole heart, mind, and strength. Audio-visual aids are now common stock in trade in our public schools and Sunday Schools. Many educational experiments have demonstrated tangibly and conclusively that a considerably higher percentage of material can be retained meaningfully when the two senses of hearing and sight are combined. The ratio goes up in proportion to the kinds and amount of involvement of the whole person in the learning process.

The symbolic action in the liturgical approach to worship has received added support from unexpected sources. John Dewey pioneered the modern version of "learning by doing"; and in spite of some over-enthusiastic extremists, the basic principle of active involvement and participation in "acting out" the great beliefs and issues of religious experience is still sound and practical.

Yet we must beware of treading hollowly and meaninglessly through practices whose original purposes and significance have been forgotten or discarded. Liturgical education, as well as other forms of Christian education, is a two-way process. On the one hand, liturgical practices reinforce ideas, but the symbols and rituals must be constantly re-interpreted and refilled with intelligible meaning from generation to generation. If this is not done, the Church will come to embrace empty worship patterns, the same mechanical hypocrisy to which the Scribes and Pharisees had fallen prey in Jesus' day.

When the Israelites merely plodded through their sacrifices and ceremonial practices, great prophets, like Amos and Hosea, who were spiritually sensitive, had to declare judgment against a sinful and hypocritical people. In a loud and clear voice they warned their people not to substitute sacrifices and rituals for a pure heart, a right relation to one's neighbor, and heartfelt prayer to God. Within the church there is ample opportunity through preaching, instruction, and discussion to keep the symbols alive and meaningful for each generation.

Neurotic Abuses

It is hard to think of any good and constructive act which is not capable of abuse and evil purpose if wrongly understood by a person with a neurotic or vicious motivation. Thinking back to the section on "security," the writer is reminded of the psychotic patient in a state mental hospital, who derived a real sense of security from the simple ritual of touching with his thumb every other block in the wall of the long corridor that led from his ward to the common dining room. If he missed a block and his ritual was this interrupted, he could not go ahead and eat his meal until he had compulsively gone back to the beginning and correctly completed the ritual. Others go through unrealistic hand washing ceremonies, sometimes even without water, until the skin is a crimson color. In this case, the sin is not washed away no matter how ardently the psychotic ritual is carried out. Gordon Allport states that "One of the symptoms of repressed emotion is symbolization, the representation of unconscious thoughts in acceptable forms in dreams, art, metaphor, wit, or folklore." [17] It is just as possible to ritualize something evil and destructive as something good and holy. We know how frequently we do the right thing for the wrong reason.

Yet, it is possible for a sick mind to derive great satisfaction but little healing benefit from ritualistic acts, ceremonials, and even the liturgy and Holy Communion. Otherwise, why would the middle-aged woman continue to desire forgiveness for what she calls "unpardonable sin" for thirty years, and never think of missing a church service nor absenting herself from the Lord's Table? Symbols and phantasy can be, and sometimes are, used as a retreat from reality. The liturgy may provide superficial comfort and lessen some nervous anxiety, but it cannot bring the deep relief of forgiveness and reconciliation if its spirit is abused and made to serve neurotic purposes. The liturgy is intended for salvation but can unfortunately become just another tragic symptom.

Because of the dangers of abuse, the liturgy and all rites of the church must be enacted intelligently if they are to be enacted at all. For example, if confession is minimized or brushed over lightly in preparation for receiving the Holy Communion, more harm than good may be done. For surely there is no forgiveness and true absolution without repentance and confession.

However, let not this admonition scare us. Is it not true that in all the good and wonderful gifts and blessings that our Heavenly Father bestows upon us, there is corresponding obligation that we render an honest and reponsible stewardship for the same?

Finally, we do not participate in the liturgy for hedonist or pragmatist purposes. Rather we participate in the liturgy as an appropriate means of worshiping God, and because it conforms to the intention and spirit of Holy Scripture. The liturgy is not a bag of tricks that have artifically been tacked onto the "program" of the church to make it more "effective." The liturgy is rather the natural and inevitable outgrowth of the experience of generation upon generation of believers who have been redeemed by the Son of God, and who live in continuous joy worshiping their Lord and sharing this joy in willing service to their neighbors.

Whereas liturgical usage and much symbolism typify worship in certain communions, it must be born in mind that in Protestantism, there have

[17] Gordon W. Allport, *Personality, A Psychological Interpretation* (New York: Holt, Rinehart and Winston, Inc., 1937), p. 184.

been strong traditions, with their own theological and social undergirding, that urge quite another emphasis in worship. We now turn to consider these other approaches.

THE FUNCTION OF SPONTANEOUS
AND INFORMAL EXPRESSION

Evelyn Underhill, who treated the use of liturgy and symbol so perceptively in her classic work, *Worship,* is broadminded enough to also point out the positive contributions of "Free Church Worship." [18] A few excerpts from this work explain the point of view of the so-called non-liturgical type of worship.

> . . . the living quality of the Christian revelation in its first hand impact on the soul, and consequent demand for an unhindered liberty of response . . . has always been an element in the Christian outlook; a valuable corrective of the special weaknesses inherent in stylized worship.
>
> Both the Church-idea and the Sect-idea, as Troeltsch saw, lie "within the consequences of the Gospel." Indeed they are completing opposites of that total Godward life which it reveals; and it is only the constant reassertion, both inside and outside its borders, of that vigorous spiritual realism from which Sects are born, which saves the worship of the Church from the crystallizing tendencies inherent in all formal religion. [19]

Underhill believes that the Cistercian and Franciscan movements were an attempt to recapture the needs of "single-minded, realistic devotion to the adoration of God" which did not appear to be available through the regular channels of the Church's worship. Was this not also true in large measure during the rise of the Reformation and later of the pietist movements in various countries of staid state religion? There comes a time when liturgy, because of misuse, misunderstanding, or neglect, serves more as an obstacle than as an open channel of holy communication. Much like a river that is dammed, the work of the Holy Spirit overflows the old banks and cuts new channels, for even the gates of hell cannot prevail against the work of God through His Church.

The writer's father tells a story of formal liturgy becoming so perfunctory and arbitrary as to be almost meaningless to the people in the state Church of Norway some eighty or ninety years ago. It appears that the pastor of a church did not customarily go to the cemetery to officiate at the grave. Instead a deacon would fulfill this seemingly dreary task, with the exception of actually saying the words of committal while pour-

[18] *Op. cit.*
[19] *Ibid.,* pp. 298, 299-300.

ing dirt upon the casket. Rather, a pipe was inserted to the casket and the earth filled in around it. Then·when it was convenient, the pastor would periodically make a visit to the cemetery and pour dirt down the pipes, "saying the words" over as many caskets as had been buried since his last visit. Here was literalistic fulfillment of liturgy and symbol with almost no personal contact with the real issues of the bereaved. It is no wonder that the pietist movement of Han Nielson Hauge and others spread rapidly, and that "prayer houses" were well-attended by people desiring a more personal expression of faith and reassurance through informal worship.

The same story in many variations stimulated the informal expressions of worship in Sweden through the work of Rosenius, the Swedish Baptists and Covenant, or "Mission Friends"; in Denmark through Wilhelm Beck and the "Inner Mission" movement; in Germany through Schleiermacher; and in England through the Methodists and the work of John Wesley, whose heart was "strangely warmed" at Aldersgate as it had not been by the cooler atmosphere of the state Church. On the American scene, we could cite instances from Congregationalism and the inception of the Disciples of Christ. All these groups and movements commonly felt that something was missing from their spiritual life—something that could not be provided, even with prodding and attempted reform, by the ministries and liturgies of the established Church. The leaders, among other convictions, believed that their new forms of worship were fulfilling a felt need of the people; and usually they cited scriptural evidence to justify their practices.

One need not refer to history of several centuries ago to observe this problem. The author recently heard a minister, with special responsibility for ministering to the American Indians migrating into a large city, report the following problem to a Council of Churches staff meeting. It appears there was an Indian family in which several members had been instructed, and were ready for Baptism and reception into church membership. Everything had been done to make them feel at home. They had suitable clothes for the day and all were in eager expectation of the event. As is frequently the case in well-ordered and liturgy-conscious churches, the church bulletin contained several asterisks indicating at which moments persons could be seated by the ushers. The Indian family was quite late in arriving and somehow they did not understand or appreciate the significance of order and time schedules in a closely organized society. When they could not be seated, they simply went home again—not in anger, but just somehow feeling they didn't fit in. The question was raised as to whether this might not have happened in an extremely informal "sect type" church where order is not prized, where interruptions are routine, and where spontaneity is the keynote.

Camps and Camp Meeting: Experiment in Spontaneity

Boys and girls sometimes return from a week at summer church camp with a sense that they have learned to worship God afresh. They are not new converts. Most church campers have been brought up in the Sunday School and have participated in the worship of the Church. Why do they look upon their religious experience at camp as especially meaningful? At the same time ministers may ask, "Why have these children not spoken of the regular Sunday morning worship with such enthusiasm?" It is an oversimplification to brush the problem aside as being sheer association; that is, association of the worship experiences at camp with all the fun and swimming and meeting a little girl friend to hold hands with at the camp fire.

The author experimented with this question of variety in worship while director of a youth camp for two summers. Each morning before breakfast, a formal liturgical service of Matins was conducted with robed liturgist and preacher, acolytes, and a choir in attendance at chapel. Then to supplement this experience, many other approaches to worship were dispersed throughout the day. A seminarian-counselor felt these were quite significant and described them as follows in his report:

> Yet there was also *informal* worship in many ways throughout the day: the simple table graces, sung or said together; the hymn-singing spontaneously started by the leader at the camp-fire, followed by a "thought for the day" and a friendship circle; the hymn-tune played by the trumpeter ten minutes before taps, quieting the camp down and announcing the time for cabin devotions; and the inspiring cabin devotions, handled each night by one of the campers . . . perhaps just a simple Scripture reading, followed by a "round prayer" with everyone contributing a few words of praise or petition. The campers thus learned worship as a feeling of God's presence and a trustful relationship with Him, not just as a ceremony confined to one form or place. Worship became an integral part of their camp day.[20]

The Reformation claims as one of its achievements the abolition of the wall of separation between sacred and secular. Luther held that the farmer in his tilling of the soil and the housewife in her cooking and cleaning should be able to view their vocations as worship and praise of God as much as the priest serving before the altar. This was not intended to minimize or secularize service and liturgy in the sanctuary, but rather to elevate all of life's activities to the level of worship.

[20] William Kerrick, "A Seminarian in a Camp Program," in a mimeographed report of a Summer Seminar in Christian Education at Lutheran Summer Camp, Gun Lake, Michigan, in co-operation with Wittenberg College and Hamma Divinity School, Springfield, Ohio, 1954.

This was the intention behind the various informal and rather spontaneous worship experiences in the youth camp. It was hoped that worship, gratitude to God for fun, friends, and the cool lake for swimming, a sense of the stewardship to the Creator for the world He has put at man's disposal; that all these thoughts, beliefs, and attitudes, would become a regular, frequent, and normal part of the young camper's daily experience. It was hoped that dependence on God the Creator, reconciliation through Christ with the Heavenly Father, the sanctifying influence of the Holy Spirit, would flash across the youth's consciousness here and there throughout the day and not only *during* Matins and *in* the Chapel.

Such informal worship needs guidance and interpretation as well as formal liturgy, or it can become mere sentimentality detached from the historic doctrines of the Church. It is possible for the "campfire meditation" to become gross heretical pantheism, but this is not necessary or inevitable if the Church leaders will give as much attention to it as to the ordering and conduct of the liturgical forms of worship.

E. Stanley Jones brought the Ashram method, a corporate spiritual quest, to America, since he had found it so useful in India.[21] The meetings, held at Green Lake, Wisconsin and elsewhere, were imitated and reproduced by national student groups and denominations. Protestant retreat houses such as Kirkridge in Pennsylvania, and Parishfield in Michigan, have been established to cultivate the spiritual life. "Camp Farthest Out" is another example. The Roman Catholic Church encourages its lay people to attend "retreats," which, though highly organized and closely structured, provide many opportunities for quiet periods and free meditation. One Catholic layman who attended such a retreat told the author that what he had appreciated most was a period of silence for a complete twenty-four-hour period. This had not been required, but he had chosen to impose it upon himself as a spiritual exercise. During this period, aside from some liturgical disciplines and services, he "just walked about the grounds and had a chance to meditate about God and the meaning of my life here on earth." These Ashrams, camps, retreats, and so forth seem to fill a real need in many people's lives. And, as in the case of the youthful campers mentioned above, they are frequently, if not usually, church members who are using this experience to supplement other more formal worship experiences.

The camp meetings and revivals of the last century, as well as the great popularity of the Billy Graham crusades and the success of the Canon Brian Green evangelism missions in the current century could all be cited to show the many people who are drawn to the spontaneity of

---

[21] E. Stanley Jones, *Along the Indian Road* (New York: The Abingdon Press, 1939).

such worship. Granted some the "spontaneity" was planned for, the point still remains. "There was something *different* about it."

Prayer Meeting and Mid-week Service in the Local Church

John and Charles Wesley belonged to a group of serious young gentlemen at Oxford called "The Holy Club," which met for prayer, meditation, and study. Later, John Wesley used this small-group method to supplement his preaching services.

> Wesley gathered people together into societies, and within different societies he organized "classes." These classes were small groups of persons, a dozen or so in number, who met regularly to confess their sins and to share their religious experiences one with the other under the guidance of some local leader. They were something in the nature of spiritual clinics, which under wise leadership had great possibilities for usefulness.[22]

Established churches have minimized or completely given up prayer circles, mid-week meetings, less formal Sunday evening services, and Bible study groups. One wonders whether there might not be a correlation between that fact and the rise of many small sects which offer these very experiences for sharing spontaneous and informal worship.

McCabe was so convinced of this need for small group fellowship and informal worship that he resolved, in the words of one of his chapter headings, to "Take the Prayer Meeting to Them." [23] After all, Jesus did not hesitate to use wedding feasts, dinner parties, and casual social contacts as opportunities for his ministry of miracle, teaching, and confrontation with the Kingdom of Heaven. Pastor McCabe arranged to have about twenty people from the church, who lived in convenient proximity, invited to the home of one of the members in that neighborhood area. The first part of the evening was given over to refreshments and socializing since many of these people had not become personally acquainted in the large church services. Then the pastor would begin to direct the conversation to deeper issues and spiritual matters. After thanking the host and hostess, he made this transition:

---

[22] Boisen, *op. cit.*, p. 123. See the entire Chapter 8, "From Sect to Church: a Case Study," for an excellent study in the change of emphasis and methods in the history of the Methodist Church. Boisen says in part, "It became thus a body of believers banded firmly together on the basis of a shared experience and a common faith which they accepted as absolute. It has now become a *church* (as opposed to a sect) with fairly prosperous membership made up chiefly of those who have been born in Methodist homes. And in the process vision and enthusiasm have been converted into habit and custom. . . . The old emotionalism has largely disappeared and the services or worship are becoming more and more dignified." Pp. 132-33.

[23] *Op. cit.*, Chapter 9.

Then I led into an opinion that some people present never had it so good in terms of salary, health, children being well, and the mortgage being reduced. But I ventured the feeling that there was an emptiness in some hearts because the ultimate meaning of life couldn't be exhausted by success in these things. They were quiet, and I read Psalm Ninety, which puts the dimension of eternity into our lives and asks God to establish the work of our hands upon us.[24]

According to the pastor who tried this experiment, it was a well-received and meaningful experience. It is as natural to discuss the ethical and religious significance of one's vocation and family life and to pray about these matters, as it is to chit-chat about them in the banter of the refreshment period. The result: "Of this I am sure: scores of couples have been to 'prayer meeting' within the past few months who would never have come near the church for such a service between Sundays." [25]

All Things to All Men

If we are to consider the psychology of individual differences, which is well validated by tests and measurements as well as by simple observation, we see the necessity of providing a number of avenues to achieve any goal. Psychological test profiles have graded scales with opposite extremes and a range between in which the bulk of the population falls. (See Figure 15, page 119.)

Should we not also expect to find, as William James found, a *"variety of religious experience,"* and a corresponding variety of religious expression. Seminarians have been asked to visit a variety of worship services as a means of broadening their ecumenical viewpoint. At the one end of the scale, one reports the dignity and solemnity of the Episcopal forms; whereas, in contrast, a student describes a Pentecostal meeting in these words: "When God does 'visit' them, the individuals give joyful, emotional exclamations such as 'Amen,' 'Lord be praised,' and 'Hallelujah.' "

One cannot help but wonder whether the Church should not be able to accommodate and minister to this whole range of temperamental, emotional, and social needs. It calls for acceptance of those quite different from oneself, and perhaps this would have to begin with the ministers' and leaders' not insisting that their own temperament or religious experience be the norm for all the members. It would also call for those spiritually warm-hearted and pietistic members, who treasure the mid-week prayer meeting, not to look down upon other members of the congregation who *only*, but faithfully, worship through liturgical

24 *Ibid.*, p. 117.
25 *Ibid.*, p. 123.

means at the "holy hour" Sunday mornings. But in an age that stresses conformity, it is difficult not to try to fit everyone into one grand "right" pattern. Maybe we will have to paraphrase Paul's words about there being neither "male nor female, Jew nor Greek, bond nor free" by saying there are neither "high church nor low church, introvert nor extravert," but all are one in Christ and can share the same Church of Christ.

PREACHING AND INSTRUCTION AS PART OF WORSHIP

The importance of preaching in the total experience of worship is highlighted by the prominent place given to the pulpit in any type of church architecture. Even in the Medieval Church, which had a strong sacramental emphasis, we find the pulpit raised above the level of pews, ornately carved, and frequently covered by a large canopy. It appears that preaching and receiving the Word of God was the most important part of worship. Some define the Church as being found where the Word is rightly preached and the Sacraments rightly administered.

The architecture of many Reformed churches symbolized the "witness of the Holy Spirit in our midst" by gathering the people and the choir around the pulpit (and Communion Table) in semi-circular pews, with the choir stalls placed behind the preacher. In the divided chancel, the pulpit is still the second most conspicuous fixture next to the altar itself. Where the Word of God is recognized as a "Means of Grace" along with the Sacraments, such emphasis on preaching is altogether appropriate.

The Merger of Prophet and Priest in Christian Worship

In the days when the Children of Israel worshiped in the movable Tabernacle, and later in the magnificent Temple, the role of priest was paramount. Occasionally, prophets would attempt to reform the religious practices of the day by speaking the "Word of the Lord" in judgment and exhortation. We hear it in the scathing sarcasm of Amos, the shepherd preacher from Tekoa:

> Come to Bethel, and transgress;
>   to Gilgal, and multiply transgression;
> bring your sacrifices every morning, your tithes every
>   three days;
> offer a sacrifice of thanksgiving of that which is leavened,
>   and proclaim freewill offerings, publish them;
>   for so you love to do, O people of Israel! [26]

---

[26] *Amos* 4:4-5.

And again in the classic words of the prophet Micah:

> With what shall I come before the Lord,
>   and bow myself before God on high?
> Shall I come before him with burnt offerings,
>   with calves a year old?
> Will the Lord be pleased with thousands of rams,
>   with ten thousands of rivers of oil?
> Shall I give my first-born for my transgression,
>   the fruit of my body for the sin of my soul?'
> He has showed you, O man, what is good;
>   and what does the Lord require of you
> but to do justice, and to love kindness,
>   and to walk humbly with your God? [27]

One can easily see the great contrast between the rugged preacher Jeremiah and his rustic, acted-out sermon illustrations: the burying of the waistcloth, walking about with yoke-bars upon his neck, and comparing the nation to pottery, first workable but later fragile and easily broken; yes, the contrast between this outspoken prophet and the socially acceptable, well-clothed priests going about their appointed rituals.

During the Exile, and even more definitely after the destruction of the Temple and the dispersion of the Jews, the Children of Israel became the people of the Book. In the synagogue, the central part of worship was the reading from the Torah and the explanation thereof.

With the Christian minister conducting the service of worship, we have a merger between the roles of prophet and priest, instructor (rabbi) and liturgist. The pulpit symbolizes the prophetic element in the Christian ministry of worship. "Thus saith the Lord" encompasses both the reading of Scripture, and the preaching of that Word of the Lord to the people. Jesus accepted the following commission from Isaiah, and it is equally applicable to the modern preacher as he represents and speaks for the Church:

> The Spirit of the Lord is upon me, because he has anointed me to preach good news to the poor. He has sent me to proclaim release to the captives and recovery of sight to the blind, to set at liberty those who are oppressed, to proclaim the acceptable year of the Lord.[28]

We read that faith comes from hearing the word of God, but how shall they hear without a preacher, and that preacher must be sent. When the minister preaches, then, he speaks not for himself, but for the Church which sent him.

---

[27] *Micah* 6:6-8.
[28] *Luke* 4:18-19.

Pentecost and the Outpouring of the Holy Spirit through Preaching

Another reason for considering preaching as the mark of the Church is that on the day of Pentecost, called the birthday of the Church, a great preaching mission by Peter converted thousands. From the beginning, preaching has been considered the message of the *whole* Church, a witness to the historic faith transmitted through the Church, not an individual's unique and individualistic possession. A minister never speaks simply for himself.

> Consequently, every pastor should think well over what he should say —well and prayerfully—interpreting the verities of the faith in the light of present conditions and problems, as matters alive and cognate to his people today . . . In short, let the pastor of a parish keep his pulpit within the sphere for which it is designed—the medium for instructing and inspiring his people in those things which bear on the love of God and neighbor, as exemplified in the life of our Lord and Master.[29]

Obviously if preaching is the outpouring of the Holy Spirit upon the people, not only the preacher's needs must be borne in mind, but also the needs of the whole believing community, as well as those of the witness to the non-believing community.

One way the Church, as the sponsor of preaching, has tried to guarantee this broad program of instruction, inspiration, and explanation, is to provide a series of texts that should be covered during the course of the year. Thus, a prescribed series of themes will be covered, ranging over the Trinity, the Incarnation and Atonement, marriage and family life, sin and judgment, Resurrection and Eternal Life, the love of God and love for one's neighbor, repentance and forgiveness. The author followed such a five-year cycle in one parish and felt it served the parishioners as at least partial protection against being preached to along the lines of the pastor's pet peeves.

The liturgy itself provides a rich source of sermon themes. The *Magnificat, Nunc Dimittis, Te Deum Laudamus,* and *Benedictus* are all Canticles which will be more meaningfully sung by the people if their theological, devotional, and practical significance has been explained in sermons. The *Agnus Dei* provides an excellent theme for a series of Lenten sermons. The Invocation and the Benediction become so familiar that it may be refreshing to have the congregation think through the theological and exegetical meaning of these short passages.

Nor should the Old Testament be neglected in one's zeal to preach the Gospel. There are lessons from the patriarchs and prophets that are as

---

[29] Cornelius Joseph Holland, *The Shepherd and His Flock* (New York: David McKay Company, Inc., 1953), p. 180.

current as tomorrow's news headlines. Psychosomatic insights and mental health factors found in the Psalms and Proverbs rival the best modern research in "practical helps for living." The Gospel cannot be fully appreciated without an understanding of the Covenant of the old dispensation, the history of Israel as a Chosen People, and the prophecies of the Messiah. In fact, we can not ignore the acts of God in history either in the era of Scripture or in the experience of the Church since apostolic times. The *Te Deum Laudamus* combines them in these majestic words:

> The glorious company of the Apostles praise thee:
> The goodly fellowship of the Prophets praise thee:
> The noble army of Martyrs praise thee.
> The holy Church throughout all the world doth acknowledge thee:
>   The Father of an infinite Majesty:
>   Thine adorable true and only Son,
>   Also the Holy Ghost the Comforter.[30]

Preaching what has been called "the whole counsel of God" will assure that all the rich blessings of Scripture as well as the accumulated experience of the Church in formulating and understanding her theology will be shared with the people. Also, no strange over-emphasis or distortion of one doctrine or another will lead to schism and the proliferation of new and bigoted setcs. Theological myopia is thus avoided and the Church focuses on the Faith clearly.

Interpretation and Intellectual Needs

If the social and emotional needs of man appear to predominate in this discussion of theology in action, it is not because the author thinks that intellectual needs are insignificant or even impractical. One only needs to think of the horrifying results of the false doctrine of racial superiority among the Nazis, to know that ideas and thought systems have tremendous power for good or evil. It is small comfort to *feel good* or *belong to the group* if one is nevertheless committed to illogical, stupid, or false propositions that sow the seeds of one's own destruction.

Preaching fulfills the function of making *sense* out of the Christian faith for the average parishioner. The preacher translates the research of systematic and biblical theology into terms understood by the layman. To use the words of Saint Paul, we must be prepared to "give a reason for the faith." Naturally, we shall be on guard lest we think we should ever be able to encompass all the universe and the mind and work of the Creator within our small finite minds—that would be to commit

[30] *Service Book and Hymnal* (Minneapolis: Augsburg Publishing House, 1958), p. 133.

Adam's sin of over-ambition. But we are within our rights and responsibility to use what mind God has given us to respond to His revelation of Himself and to His will. One of the functions of preaching is to provide this rationale of the Christian faith and to apply it to the issues of daily life, and to the goal of the life to come.

Gordon Allport insists that man needs a "unifying philosophy of life" to provide balance and perspective for his life. This helps to keep all his demanding drives and competing sentiments in their proper places. Religion serves this function as its all-embracing vision rises above lesser standards and values such as the political, the economic, the aesthetic, or even the social criteria of life, thought, or action.

Just as a broad range of worship experiences should make it possible to provide for the needs of a wide range of individual temperaments within the same church; so, truly adequate preaching should challenge and stimulate the well-educated as well as offer, in the words of Saint Poul, "milk for babes." Unless it ministers to the intellect of man, the Church is not caring for the *whole* man.

It is not the purpose of this discussion to deal with homiletics—the theory and method of preaching—but only to show how preaching is an integral part of worship, and to show how it supplements the emotional and social aspects of worship. We have also wanted to stress the importance of making preaching the concern and responsibility of the whole Church. It must never become an individualistic project of the preacher for his own benefit and enjoyment as an art form, for his own personal release of gripes and tensions, nor for his own personal edification. Oh, yes, it can be excellent in literary style and so forth; but throughout all preaching one should sense the obvious fact that this is the message of God as the Church understands it. It must be instructive and inspirational for the members of the household of faith, and it must be a challenging witness to the non-believing world.

PRIVATE DEVOTION AND RELIGIOUS EXPERIENCE

Question: Do you go to church? *Answer:* I am part of the Church. But the Church does meet together, if that's what you're asking. *Question:* Where is your Church? *Answer:* Well, let's see, about this time of the morning, most of it is at work, except for those on the night shift, or those who are sick. Some are at work in this factory and that, others are working in this office or that store, some are in school, some in their kitchens, the Church is infiltrating through the whole town right now. *Question:* What does your Church do? *Answer:* I've already told you. It's spread all through the town involved in all sorts of work, doing that work in such a way and talking in such a way as to let others know what is already true: that Jesus Christ is boss of this city and all that goes on in it. This is the Church's work. And then, one day a week, we rest from our Church work and gather together to hear again our Lord speaking to us, that we may go back renewed to the task he has set before us.[31]

The above is a touching and radical statement of the fact that the Church is made up of people, not bricks. The Church is the Communion of Saints; and all the buildings, mimeograph machines, schedules and appointment books, pledge cards and envelopes, are important only as they contribute to or make more possible the salvation of individual persons. If this is true, worship does not cease with the organ postlude one Sunday morning at 12:00 and begin again with the choir processional the following Sunday at 11:00 A.M.

Again, using the words of the *Te Deum Laudamus,* "To thee Cherubim and Seraphim *continually* do cry." We, like the angels, should worship God continually, and, according to Scripture, "pray without ceasing." This is the true test of whether or not we have broken down the wall of separation between "secular" and "sacred" spheres of life. Scripture is full of this emphasis:

Let not the sun go down on thy wrath (*daily confession*)
The Pharisee and publican in prayer (*one's own private prayer life*)
Need for the "daily drowning of the Old Adam" (*forgiveness*)
Jesus in prayer "apart" in the Garden of Gethsemane and elsewhere.
The good Samaritan (*spontaneous acts of love toward neighbor*)
Is any one among you suffering? Let him pray. Is any cheerful? Let him
    sing praise.
O Lord, my God, I call for help by day;
    I cry out in the night before thee. (*We may call upon God any time.*)
Let my prayer come before thee,
    incline thy ear to my cry!
Unless the Lord builds the house,
    those who build it labor in vain. (*No activity should be undertaken
    without God's blessing.*)
Unless the Lord watches over the city,
    the watchman stays awake in vain.

There are many more passages showing that God and His worship are not confined to the Sabbath nor to the Temple.

Churches have become aware of this need to foster worship and spiritual life between Sundays. Over twenty-five thousand small hymn books with devotional readings and prayers for family devotions were distributed by one group to families while on their summer vacations. Families are encouraged to make and use Advent wreaths with brief devotions in the pre-Christmas season. Daily devotional guides such as

[31] Paul M. van Buren, "The New Biblical Theology in Parish Life," in *Religion in Life,* Vol. 28, No. 4, Autumn, 1959, pp. 535-36.

The Upper Room are circulated by the millions to encourage private and family devotions. All of this attention to the spiritual and devotional life of the individual believer is a necessary and natural obligation of the total Church in its worship life.

Increasingly, the churches have interpreted the layman's "secular" vocations as the service of God, and as a response to the gifts of grace through Christ. For, after all, the worship of God goes on through individual hearts and lives, not as an abstraction.

We come back to our original theme. Worship is the central mission of the Church, and the Church must pursue this holy task from as many vantage points and through as many channels as possible, liturgical and spontaneous, corporate and individual.

CHAPTER 3

THE SETTING
OF THE PARISH

We have considered the theological and sociological nature of the Church in general and its holy work of worship. Now we must turn to the church in specific as it is represented tangibly at the local level, and every church has a location, a setting.

How can we become objective and factual about any setting in which we are personally involved? A photograph of oneself is more likely to be objective than a self-description of whether one is handsome or homely. A floor plan is more dependable than a real estate agent's description of the lake cottage for sale and the "real big picture window." A budget is more accurate than one's guess that it shouldn't cost too much, because "figures don't lie." The same difficulty and, therefore, the same necessity for objective analysis pertains to the church and community of which one is a participating and emotionally involved member.

For the approach to the church and community that follows, the author is indebted to a wide range of sociologists of religion, urban planning leaders, social research, and church survey workers.[1] A growing

---

[1] The author is indebted for examples of such research to Walter Kloetzli, Jr., of the National Lutheran Council, Harold W. Baldwin of the Presbyterian Board of National Missions, John L. Mixon of McCormick Seminary, Murray H. Leiffer of Garrett Biblical Institute, Bureau of Social and Religious Research, Joseph B. Schuyler, S. J., of Fordham University, and Joseph H. Fichter, S. J., author of many writings in this field including *Southern Parish: Dynamics of a City Church,* to mention only a few workers in this field.

experience in this field has made consultation available to most any church which wishes help in understanding the *setting* of its parish.

THE "COMMUNITY" OR AREA OF RESPONSIBILITY

There are many ways in which we can step outside of our community and look upon it with helpful detachment. If one has the good fortune to fly over his community in an airplane or helicopter, he suddenly sees things in different perspective. Areas such as lakes, school yards, playgrounds, factories and railroad yards, parking lots and shopping centers, as well as various groups of homes appear to be larger or smaller than he had expected, farther apart or more compactly grouped than he expected.

The civil engineer's trained eye visualizes the same thing from his contour maps and elevation figures. The map maker and city planner have made it their profession to look for the objective landmarks and characteristics that identify the nature of the community. Just as the medical student spends some time studying the skeleton of the body, so the student of a community must begin with the geography, landscape, streets, and buildings before he clothes this basic frame with flesh and blood and finally tries to assess the "personality" of the community. He needs to know something about the context, limitations of setting, advantages of environment within which the dynamic life and interaction of the community are played out. Every drama takes place in some setting, in some place, and at some moment in time.

On the following two pages are maps of the same setting in a part of Minneapolis: [2] Figure 1 shows the way the community *has been* used, the types of buildings and activities such as recreational facilities, industrial areas, and residential functions needed; Figure 2 shows the *proposed usage* of this land, predicted by zoning ordinances, economic, and other facts. These maps compared show the direction this community is moving—the shape of things to come. Note the implications of this development for the church marked by a cross in census tract 88. This particular church faced the prospect of having ninety of its families dislocated if all the area listed as zoned for heavy industry were to be transferred to that purpose from its present residential use. Since these maps were drawn, a completely separate and new factor, super-highway construction, had to be taken into consideration; another large number of families will be relocated. These factors indicate the urgent need for

[2] David Belgum, *A Good Look at Our Church*, a report of a survey made of Holy Trinity Lutheran Church, 28th Ave. So., and 31st St. E., Minneapolis, Minnesota, Spring, 1956, by David Belgum.

LAND USAGE 1948
EAST SECTION SOUTH MINNEAPOLIS

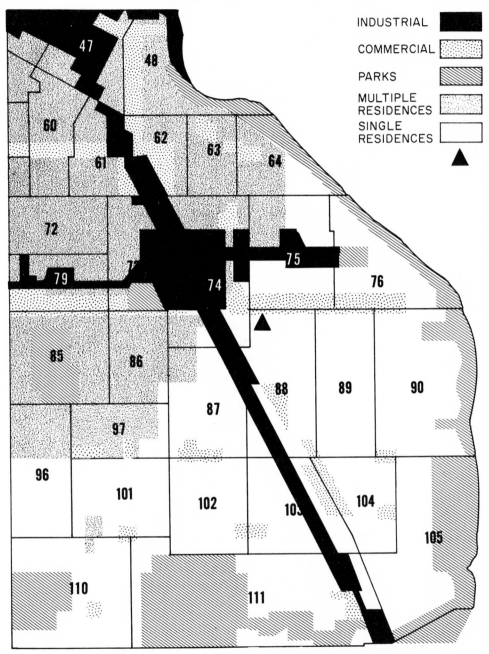

INDUSTRIAL

COMMERCIAL

PARKS

MULTIPLE
RESIDENCES

SINGLE
RESIDENCES

Figure 1.

LAND USAGE PROPOSED
EAST SECTION SOUTH MINNEAPOLIS

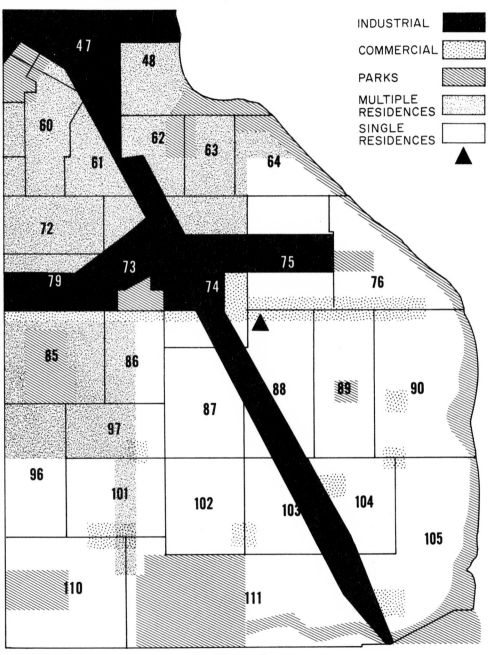

INDUSTRIAL

COMMERCIAL

PARKS

MULTIPLE RESIDENCES

SINGLE RESIDENCES

Figure 2.

assessing the trends and possible developments of a community or neighborhood, as well as its present condition. The rate of change has accelerated more in our generation than previously, and it has a direct bearing on the local church.

The term "community" is deliberately put in quotation marks because its meaning has changed. New factors in transportation and social relations have made "community of interest" perhaps as important as, or more significant than, the older concept of the geographic community. It is not unusual for a housewife to drive five miles to shop at her favorite supermarket. Her husband's recreational activities may be more influenced by the fact that his factory has a bowling team, which bowls every Tuesday night across town, than by the fact that they live across the street from a playground, which has a ball diamond, skating rink, or picnic ground. The school bus may take the children to a large consolidated school where friends are made as easily from a distance as with children next door. The rapid rate at which people move from one job and city to another adds to this weakening of what formerly were community ties and community interests in the geographic sense. How different from the "good old days" when work, play, education, shopping, and maybe even relatives, were within walking distance and one seldom needed to venture beyond the confines of one's own community! What's more, these same developments are beginning to apply to the rural communities as well as to the large cities.[3]

Each church must deliberately analyze and select its area of responsibility rather than drift along the paths of least resistance. If it chooses some other basis than the old "parish boundary" of so-and-so many square city blocks, then it should be able to verbalize what that area of responsibility is and state how it shall be served. Just a few such examples might be cited: the church specializing in student work near a university campus, one ministering in a particular way to a military post with its service men and their families, or the church witnessing in the business district where very few people live but where multitudes mill about. Whatever the area of responsibility or community served, let it not be arrived at by default, but by deliberate decision and bold planning appropriate to the needs of that community.

This discussion should not leave the reader with the impression that

[3] John E. Seeley, R. Alexander Sim, and Elizabeth W. Loosley, *Crestwood Heights* (New York: Basic Books, Inc., 1956), Chapter 11, "The Club: Sociality." This and other studies of suburban living indicate that great mobility makes transient suburbanites hunger for a feeling of local belonging and a sense of community. Sometimes, they throw themselves into the task of creating a "community" with almost compulsive zeal.

See also *The Organization Man* by William H. Whyte, Jr. (Garden City, New York: Doubleday & Co., Inc., 1956), Part VII, "The New Suburbia," and *Love and Conflict* by Gibson Winter (Garden City, New York: Doubleday & Company, Inc., 1958).

just because a *special* community of interest is being served, a church is freed from responsibility to its neighborhood community. The issue was raised merely to show the complexity of the parish setting and also to suggest that no glib answers or easy solutions are possible.

The survey of this particular church, revealed that, whereas its large membership is primarily drawn from a relatively compact circle with a 1½ mile radius from the church, only 27 per cent of the members indicated that "location" was a factor in their deciding to affiliate with that church. Another 17 per cent of the membership were attracted to the church by some friend or personal association. Among the youth who belong to the church, 78 per cent of those who lived less than ½ mile from the church participated in the youth groups. The percentages were almost the same for other more distant groups:

½ to 1 mile	43 out of a possible 53 or 82%
1 to 2 miles	31 out of a possible 42 or 74%
Over 2 miles	34 out of a possible 43 or 79%

This is enough to suggest that an analysis of boundaries such as lakes, rivers, railroad lines, super-highways, hills, swamps, or physical equipment such as buildings and utilities, condition of streets, and vacant lots, influential as they may be, do not suffice to give a full picture of a community today. We turn next to the people who act upon this stage and about whom the church is chiefly concerned.

THE NATURE AND NEEDS OF THIS COMMUNITY

Once we have determined the area of our responsibility, we can focus our attention on even more specific questions concerning people. It is quite noble to say, "The world is my parish," but most of us are limited by time and space to making our contribution and rendering our service in a particular place with all its limitations.

In gathering data about the needs of a community, it is good to use standard units of measurements in order to keep statistics comparable and to utilize more readily information that has been gathered by other workers. Therefore, the study of a parish should use census tracts as geographic units. A wealth of information is already available broken down into such small areas. Such maps can usually be obtained in quantity free or at a nominal cost from the local city Traffic Division, City Engineer's Office, or Voter's Registration Office.

Every ten years the U. S. Census Bureau publishes detailed information in census tracts. Such items are included as the following: population density per acre, age groups, number of persons receiving public assistance per census tract, characteristics of housing, showing physical condition, type, facilities, and whether rented or self-owned.

Police statistics and community welfare research departments provide a variety of information in different metropolitan areas. Here the unit of measurement may likely be by police precincts. It is important to know both the number of arrests and violations by area of *incident* and area of *residence of offender*, which may be quite different. These figures will also be broken down by sex, month (to show peak periods of trouble), and whether committed by adults or juveniles.

Lest we become so bogged down with statistics that we cannot see the forest for the trees, it may be helpful to provide more general or summary information as a way of interpreting the nature and needs of a community to the members of the congregation.

Today researchers can classify areas of a city very accurately according to their particular social problems or needs. The Research Department, Community Welfare Council, Community Chest and Council of Hennepin County, Minnesota, have collected information that is compiled on the map in Figure 3, entitled "Potential Social Need Index—1950" (the year the last census was available). Social need was determined by nine factors: income, mobility, overcrowding, relief rate, juvenile delinquency, population density, infant mortality, education, and dependent age. These are factors which greatly influence the community and the lives of the individuals with whom Holy Trinity Church is working (located in the upper edge of census tract 88).

Notice that within a few blocks of the Cross of Holy Trinity Church there exists all five of the social need groups: 89 has least social need, 87 below average, 88 average, 73 above average, and 74 has the greatest level of social need in the city together with the other solid black areas one typically encounters as one draws closer to the center of any large city. Such clear cut objective presentation of evidence can clarify to a parish its unique situation more than verbal generalizations.

This church is in the middle of the full range of social and economic extremes. Wonderful! Unfortunately, many churches cannot take this kind of tension and soon drift toward a one-class group neglecting all others. Holy Trinity has a unique opportunity to provide fellowship and service which cross all social, cultural, and economic lines in the name of Him who prayed in His high priestly prayer, "that they all may be one." Other churches frequently find themselves in a community that is homogeneous in socio-economic strength and even housing facilities. This is most obviously seen in the rapidly expanding suburbs.

Here again the statistics are not an end in themselves, but a means to help correct our errors in subjective judgment. Most of us develop prejudices about our communities and home towns which do not always conform to the facts. So we say, "It's a middle class town," or "A lot of old

POTENTIAL SOCIAL NEED INDEX 1950

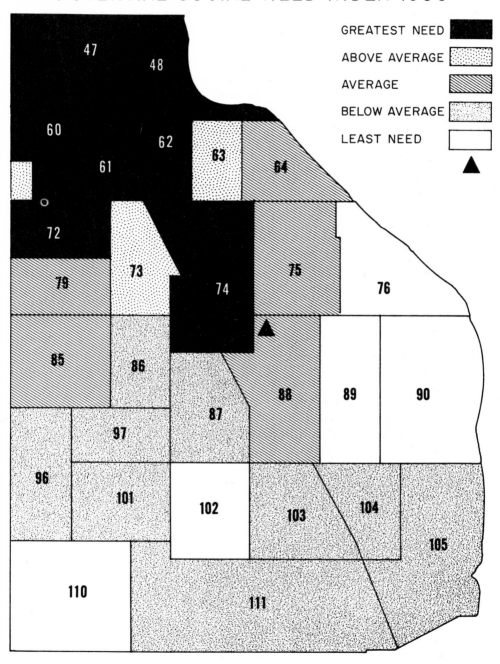

Figure 3.

people live out our way," or "Have you noticed how many children there are around our neighborhood?" or "People seem to be moving around more now than they used to," or "There certainly has been an epidemic of juvenile delinquency lately." These guesses are not accurate enough. No supermarket would locate its stores nor a gasoline company place its stations on such rough estimates of a community. Business today wants facts before it plans and invests time and money in any project. Neither can the Church afford wide margins of error when people are ready and willing to share objective information about the community in which we work, worship, and serve.

Sociologists have developed a most interesting diagram called the "population pyramid" in which the two factors of age and sex are related in exact percentages.[4] A theoretical pyramid or equilateral triangle is the basic pattern because in an average cross-section of the population there will be more people in the lower age brackets and fewer and fewer persons in the upper age brackets until the graph narrows to a point among the ninety-year-olds or those who reach a hundred.

Changes in the birth rate, however, usually prevent this graph from being a true equilateral triangle. Immigration and special working conditions may also tend to make a given age group bulge out on the graph for a given community as compared with the population statistics of the whole country. In Figure 4, low birth rate could account for the small percentage of persons between ages 5 and 20. The offspring of the war-time marriage boom could account for the sharp increase in the number of children born between 1945 and 1950. Also, many workers above the age of 20 are drained off from the outlying rural areas and attracted to industrial jobs in the city. A rural parish in upper-eastern Wisconsin reported very few post-highschool young adults in its membership since they had gone to Milwaukee and Chicago and other cities to find employment. In using such statistics one must be cautious of making generalizations.

Is the church ministering to the kinds of people that are in its area of responsibility? If the population pyramid of the parish bears little or no resemblance to the pyramid of the community, there is real need for self-examination. In Figure 5 are a few samples of how remarkably dissimilar various communities can be.[5]

There is no attempt here to indicate how a given church should react to its community; the purpose of this discussion is simply to encourage any church to be *aware* of its community. The assumption is that the first step in solving a problem or meeting a need is to be aware of the situa-

---

[4] Newcomb, Charles Shelton, "A Single Numerical Index of Age and Sex Distribution of Population," Unpublished M. A. thesis, Department of Sociology, University of Chicago, 1930.
[5] Newcomb, *op. cit.*

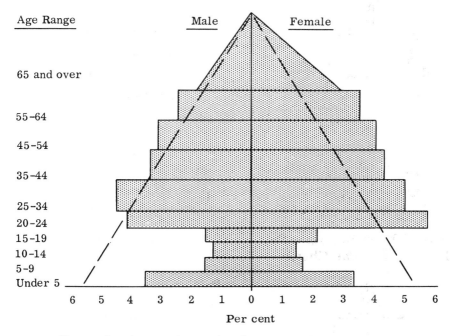

Figure 4. Age and sex distribution of the population of census tract 5-C, St. Louis, Missouri, 1950.[5]

tion in all its complex and interlocking dynamics. But the Church is not the only social institution in the community, nor is it the only one that is keenly concerned about the problems and needs of the people that live there.

OTHER AGENCIES AS PARTNERS IN SERVICE

Many agencies in the community have staff members serving the needs of people out of a deep and true Christian motivation, a sense of Christian vocation. Many of these workers are active members of churches in the communities in which they work, or in neighboring communities. According to van Buren, these workers might be said to be the Church at work in a very real sense. Therefore, we are not stretching a point to say that many constructive agencies in the community are partners in service with the Church, especially in the sphere of carrying out the command of Christ to "love thy neighbor as thyself."

There are many community agencies and resources which overlap some of the aims of the Church in serving the needs of people. There was a time when the parish routinely included the church, school, hospital

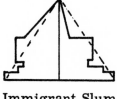

Immigrant Slum

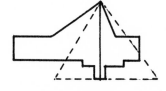

Transient Hotel - Loop

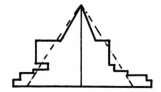

Area of First Immigrant
Settlement - The Ghetto

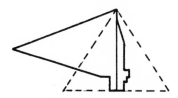

Lodging-house Hotel-
Hobo Area

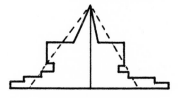

Area of Second Immigrant
Settlement

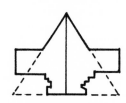

Rooming-house Area

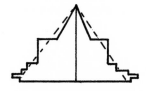

Area of Third Immigrant
Settlement

Residence Hotel Area

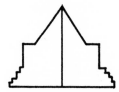

Area of Workingmen's Homes

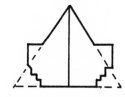

Apartment House Area

Figure 5. Age and sex distributions in various
neighborhoods.[6]

and all other "welfare" services. Today most of these functions have been shared with city, county, state, federal, and private welfare agencies. The commission: "Bear ye one another's 'burdens and so fulfill the law of Christ," is no longer the sole responsibility of the Church, but is shared with other agencies.

No conclusive list can be drawn up that applies to all communities; each church must look about in its own community to make such a catalogue. In a study entitled "Community Teamwork," Harold J. Belgum discovered how little communication there was between social service workers and other public servants in the compact Glenwood community of North Minneapolis comprising only two census tracts (the majority of which has now been completely torn down and redeveloped in a slum clearance program of urban renewal).

> *Two Hundred and Twenty Friendly Strangers.* When the directory was finally completed it contained well over two hundred names, twice the number that had been anticipated by those who "knew best." As the year progressed and the worker came to know a representative sample of thirty of these persons, he found that *they did not know one another.* This was true not only between fields of work. Another significant fact was that they did not know the community, they did not know its strengths, its resources, nor did they know the implications of its problems. So they could really be called "strangers." But all of them were above the average in friendliness, eagerness to learn about the community. And they were filled with a genuine desire to help those who needed help. So they could be called "friendly" as well as "strangers." [6]

One can easily see how this comes to pass. Each worker is "snowed under" with work, reports, board and committee meetings (since many of these are "voluntary" organizations). In fact, if a pastor does not deliberately seek out and meet some of these workers early in his pastorate, he too can become so caught up in the whirl of his schedule that years may pass before he meets by chance those others who are working intimately with his own people.

As a student of community organization, the author lists four categories of community worker concerned about human welfare:

1. Those who help preserve the spiritual, cultural, and intellectual values.
2. Those who maintain and promote health and welfare.
3. Those who cultivate and maintain relationships and communications.
4. Those who are concerned with emergencies and dangers.[7]

[6] Harold J. Belgum, "Community Teamwork," A Field Work Project at Wells Memorial, 1950-1951. An unpublished paper submitted to the University of Minnesota School of Social Work, p. 5.
[7] Harold J. Belgum, *loc. cit.*

Obvious agencies are the schools, parks and playgrounds, settlement houses, YMCA branches, hospitals, and out-patient clinics, both of the general-surgical and mental health types, Scouting organizations or 4-H clubs, and the like. Less obvious are the Visiting Nurse Service, family and children's social service agencies, county welfare board, whose offices may not be in the immediate community, but whose service is as available as the nearest telephone, and whose professional personnel may be quietly going about their duties in our midst. How often a pastor or parishioner has said, after a problem has come and gone, "I wish I had known about that service before."

We could go on to mention librarians, the city or state council of Protestant churches, even denominational agencies, which could go by the board unlisted just because they were so self-evident.

No one person should attempt to compile such a list, because his special interests or lack of contacts may leave whole groups untouched. This is a list that should grow over several months and in consultation with other community leaders.

There is a double reason for enumerating and bringing into community and parish awareness the agencies suggested above. The one is to receive help when needs of parishioners arise, specialized help to which referral can be made by the pastor or other member of the congregation. The second reason is motivated by Christian love and the inevitable desire to serve one's neighbor that must flow from that love. A fair share of the church's volunteer efforts should be devoted to aiding these agencies in their works of mercy. Red Cross Grey Ladies are needed in the hospitals. Young and old, sick and unfortunate, can all be ministered to by modern "good Samaritans" co-ordinating their efforts through such agencies.

By clearing through authorized agencies, often much unnecessary duplication and wasted effort can be avoided. Love and mercy need not be any less genuine and spontaneous because they are channeled to where they can do the most good and be properly administered. Many a "do-gooder" could have avoided embarrassment and unnecessary criticism by having co-operated with a reputable agency instead of going off on an isolated and individualized "project."

Lastly, because it is so often forgotten, any parish survey must include a full description of the sister churches in the community. Where are they located? What is their scope and program? Is there any natural place for co-ordinating our efforts? How can we avoid needless "competition" in the bad sense? These questions apply to evangelism, Christian education, youth work programs, special service projects, and local community projects wherever the spiritual and moral life of the people is at stake and wherever co-operation makes more sense than going it alone.

We have considered the setting of the parish not out of idle sociological curiosity but to equip ourselves better for the work of the Church. Yet, before considering the mission of the Church, we need to focus attention as through a microscope on the Church as a living social organism as well as a social entity with structure and form. We need to ask what the local congregation is actually like. Within the setting of the drama, who are the actors and what are their relationships to each other as they participate in the plot?

CHAPTER 4

THE STRUCTURE
OF THE CONGREGATION

Now that the setting is clearly understood, we can focus more specifically upon the local church itself. We can ask historical and analytical questions about how and why one particular church happened to be where and what it is. What are the factors that have molded its character and shaped its program? What administrative and organizational structure has it found necessary to develop in carrying out its work; and wherein are these external forms and patterns truly representative to its inner life?

PRELUDE TO THE PRESENT SCENE

Too often a church waits for its twenty-fifth, fiftieth, or hundredth anniversary to take stock of its historical origins and development. The author is indebted to Professor S. C. Kincheloe of the Chicago Theological Seminary, a pioneer in the church survey field, for the following pertinent questions:

"Under what circumstances was it founded? What was the character of its leaders from stage to stage? What have been the chief stages of its life? What special crises has it had? Where does it stand now with reference to its past history; i.e., is it at its greatest strength or has it been stronger and declined? Does the history of the church reflect basic

56

changes in the nature of its community and constituency?" [1] (*from a mimeographed outline*)

It is not enough to say in disgust, "I can't understand why the charter members built the church at the end of this narrow street—what stupid planning." The author recalls tracing back the old platte maps in Boston and discovering that at one time a particular church and steeple had been quite prominent among low, modest residences and had become obscured only in later years by three and four-story apartment houses and tenements. Such an historical background survey will not only increase one's tolerance for predecessors but will also alert a person to the dynamic and ever-changing nature of the community in which one is carrying out the work of the Church. In the next forty years there will surely be even greater changes than in the past forty years. Protestants frequently envy the perspective of their Roman Catholic neighbors in terms of long range planning and development; perhaps it is due to their respect for history and their orientation to think in terms of centuries instead of decades.

Has this church been related to or has it sponsored certain projects over the years, such as providing chaplaincy and worship services to a local home for the aged or other institution, aiding in the relocation of a considerable number of displaced persons, offering the use of its facilities to outside groups, etc.? Did the church originally serve an ethnic or special language group and subsequently change its character over the years? What has been the "reputation" of the congregation in the community? Is it associated with a certain class of society; upper, middle, or lower? Is it known for its aloofness or its co-operation in inter-church and denominational enterprises? One can trace its membership growth and various financial trends by simple line graphs. Getting reactions from older members as to what the "ups and downs" mean can be helpful.

Ultimately one wants to come down to the present scene, which may be composed of at least three factors: the people, the program, and the place (or as the church building is sometimes crassly called, "the plant"). Let us begin with the place. It is not enough to study the floor plan of the church to understand it. One must inquire into the uses and purposes of the various areas and rooms. One must distinguish types as well as frequency. Some areas are used 1-3 hours per week (perhaps the nave of the church, and only for worship); occasional meeting rooms may be occupied 4-10 hours per week; others as many as 15-20 hours per week; and the offices may be in almost constant use for 50 or more hours per week. These differences can be graphically represented on a floor plan

---

[1] S. C. Kincheloe, "Selected Outline for the Study of a Local Church," from *Church and Community Studies,* an undated, mimeographed outline.

by shading the various areas in different tones or patterns. Some churches have been singled out for criticism in this whole area because of ineffective utilization of space and facilities, and failure to exercise good stewardship of their property.

Sample activities schedules or calendars should be studied on a weekly or monthly basis. These should be selected from different seasons of the year. It may be sufficient to chart the activities from a typical week in the fall, during Lent, and again in the summer. The duplication and over-crowding of the activities schedule thus becomes quite obvious. To avoid certain unhealthy competitions and hyper-activism on the part of some over-zealous extroverts, it may be advisable to schedule two activities at the same time and thus force a choice. Some churches have put a limit on the amount of leadership or responsibility that one person (and maybe one family) shall be allowed. That would avoid situations where either husband or wife, or both, are "at a church meeting" eight or nine nights in a row—and sometimes with young children left alone in the homes of these "absentee parents." "Family Night" programs have been developed as a specific outgrowth of such a schedule study.

Finally, the church building should be analyzed from the outside as to access, appearance, and the impression it makes on "outsiders." This must include the increasingly important question of parking space. One's imagination must also survey the immediate area for possible expansion space if needed, which might involve the acquisition of land and the prevention of encroachment by adverse establishments.

CHARACTER OF THE CONSTITUENCY

Members of the congregation are first and foremost individuals and they should never be lost sight of in the modern crowd psychology of "the herd." Yet, the fact remains that people in the church act as members of certain groups or tend to cluster around common interests or characteristics. Thus certain persons gravitate toward Boy Scouts not only because of their age and sex but because of their interest, just as others are drawn toward the choir because of their interest in music, and still others are bound closer together because of vocational or recreational interests held in common. Therefore, it is not a violation of the dignity of the individual to inquire into his personal characteristics, skills, interests, or needs.

The age-sex distribution of the congregation is significant when compared with the same proportion and percentages of the population pyramid of the community which it serves (see Figures 4 and 5). If the elderly persons in the community are not proportionally represented in the congregation, certain penetrating questions need to be asked; the same is true for children, middle-aged persons, men, women, or any other grouping. Dot maps of the adult membership and parish education enrollment should be constructed to indicate which census tracts will be considered the "community" of this church.

Some systematic and convenient method for collecting and correlating these statistics must be used that is not too complicated and yet makes the necessary data available and capable of ready reference. One method, Keysort,[2] has been found useful in businesses and educational institutions where large assortments of facts need to be readily available for personnel directors, deans, advisors, program directors, and so on. The method or system, per se, is not as important as getting the job done, and there are many systems and devices that can provide correlated data. The data-gathering procedure should be comprehensive and simple at the same time. Some churches have installed elaborate systems only to give them up soon afterward because they were too complex or expensive to maintain.

One such parish survey card used by a variety of Protestant churches is shown in Figure 6.[3] Such a card is conveniently filled out by callers in the annual "Every Member Visitation" in either the evangelism or stewardship program of the congregation. A few interesting correlations may appear. Perhaps the financial support as well as the participation falls within certain age ranges or among those who have belonged to this church for a minimum of x number of years. What does this tabulation tell about the mobility of the people, the ratio of self-owned to rental dwellings? Is there a small clustering of members who participate in many (perhaps too many) activities—in short, how broad is the base of active participation and willingness to volunteer for service? These could also be distributed on a small population pyramid and represented on a dot map to show whether the "leaders" come from the same general area as the "rest of the members."

Joseph B. Schuyler, S. J., Professor of Sociology at Fordham University, discusses this method in connection with a most thorough survey he made of a Roman Catholic parish in the Bronx, New York.

Notice that the interest here is in finding *groups* with which to work, the groups with similar interests, needs, and capabilities. Through them parish policy can be organized in the way required by the apostolate in a society of mass population. This is what Pope Pius XI meant when he said that "The individual apostolate is no longer (if it ever was) adequate."

[2] Trade Mark Registered with the United States Patent Office by The McBee Company, Athens, Ohio.

[3] This card grew out of the author's experience in the Holy Trinity survey and in response to requests from pastors for help in conducting their own parish self-studies.

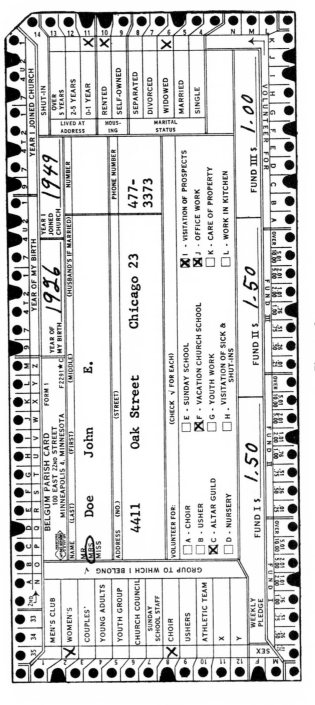

Figure 6.

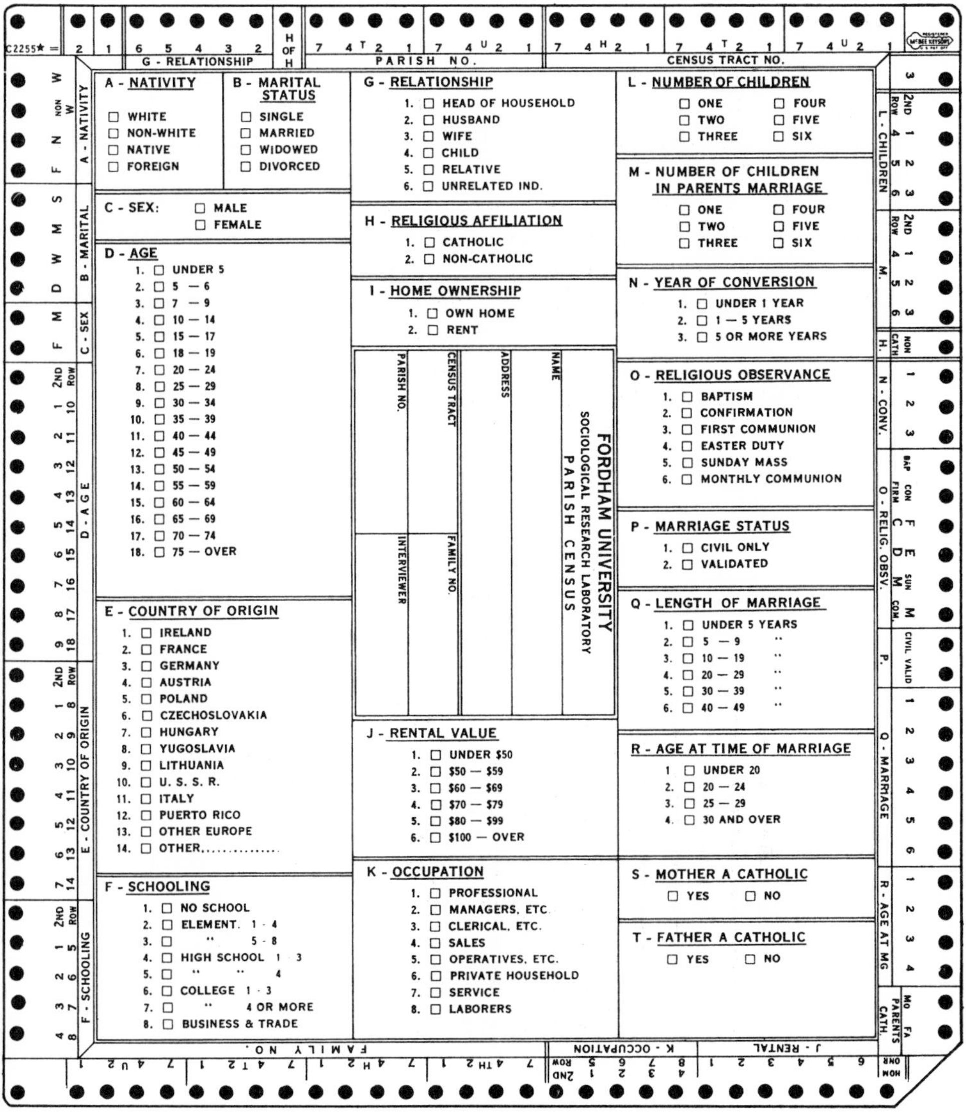

FORDHAM UNIVERSITY
SOCIOLOGICAL RESEARCH LABORATORY
PARISH CENSUS

PARISH NO. | CENSUS TRACT | ADDRESS | NAME | INTERVIEWER | FAMILY NO.

A - NATIVITY
☐ WHITE
☐ NON-WHITE
☐ NATIVE
☐ FOREIGN

B - MARITAL STATUS
☐ SINGLE
☐ MARRIED
☐ WIDOWED
☐ DIVORCED

C - SEX: ☐ MALE ☐ FEMALE

D - AGE
1. ☐ UNDER 5
2. ☐ 5 — 6
3. ☐ 7 — 9
4. ☐ 10 — 14
5. ☐ 15 — 17
6. ☐ 18 — 19
7. ☐ 20 — 24
8. ☐ 25 — 29
9. ☐ 30 — 34
10. ☐ 35 — 39
11. ☐ 40 — 44
12. ☐ 45 — 49
13. ☐ 50 — 54
14. ☐ 55 — 59
15. ☐ 60 — 64
16. ☐ 65 — 69
17. ☐ 70 — 74
18. ☐ 75 — OVER

E - COUNTRY OF ORIGIN
1. ☐ IRELAND
2. ☐ FRANCE
3. ☐ GERMANY
4. ☐ AUSTRIA
5. ☐ POLAND
6. ☐ CZECHOSLOVAKIA
7. ☐ HUNGARY
8. ☐ YUGOSLAVIA
9. ☐ LITHUANIA
10. ☐ U. S. S. R.
11. ☐ ITALY
12. ☐ PUERTO RICO
13. ☐ OTHER EUROPE
14. ☐ OTHER..............

F - SCHOOLING
1. ☐ NO SCHOOL
2. ☐ ELEMENT. 1 - 4
3. ☐ " 5 - 8
4. ☐ HIGH SCHOOL 1 - 3
5. ☐ " " 4
6. ☐ COLLEGE 1 - 3
7. ☐ " 4 OR MORE
8. ☐ BUSINESS & TRADE

G - RELATIONSHIP
1. ☐ HEAD OF HOUSEHOLD
2. ☐ HUSBAND
3. ☐ WIFE
4. ☐ CHILD
5. ☐ RELATIVE
6. ☐ UNRELATED IND.

H - RELIGIOUS AFFILIATION
1. ☐ CATHOLIC
2. ☐ NON-CATHOLIC

I - HOME OWNERSHIP
1. ☐ OWN HOME
2. ☐ RENT

J - RENTAL VALUE
1. ☐ UNDER \$50
2. ☐ \$50 — \$59
3. ☐ \$60 — \$69
4. ☐ \$70 — \$79
5. ☐ \$80 — \$99
6. ☐ \$100 — OVER

K - OCCUPATION
1. ☐ PROFESSIONAL
2. ☐ MANAGERS, ETC.
3. ☐ CLERICAL, ETC.
4. ☐ SALES
5. ☐ OPERATIVES, ETC.
6. ☐ PRIVATE HOUSEHOLD
7. ☐ SERVICE
8. ☐ LABORERS

L - NUMBER OF CHILDREN
☐ ONE ☐ FOUR
☐ TWO ☐ FIVE
☐ THREE ☐ SIX

M - NUMBER OF CHILDREN IN PARENTS MARRIAGE
☐ ONE ☐ FOUR
☐ TWO ☐ FIVE
☐ THREE ☐ SIX

N - YEAR OF CONVERSION
1. ☐ UNDER 1 YEAR
2. ☐ 1 — 5 YEARS
3. ☐ 5 OR MORE YEARS

O - RELIGIOUS OBSERVANCE
1. ☐ BAPTISM
2. ☐ CONFIRMATION
3. ☐ FIRST COMMUNION
4. ☐ EASTER DUTY
5. ☐ SUNDAY MASS
6. ☐ MONTHLY COMMUNION

P - MARRIAGE STATUS
1. ☐ CIVIL ONLY
2. ☐ VALIDATED

Q - LENGTH OF MARRIAGE
1. ☐ UNDER 5 YEARS
2. ☐ 5 — 9 "
3. ☐ 10 — 19 "
4. ☐ 20 — 29 "
5. ☐ 30 — 39 "
6. ☐ 40 — 49 "

R - AGE AT TIME OF MARRIAGE
1 ☐ UNDER 20
2. ☐ 20 — 24
3. ☐ 25 — 29
4. ☐ 30 AND OVER

S - MOTHER A CATHOLIC
☐ YES ☐ NO

T - FATHER A CATHOLIC
☐ YES ☐ NO

Figure 7.

The numerically complete, informationally extensive and administratively maneuverable census can alone uncover these uniformities, these collective objectives and organizable agencies of the parish apostolate. Such a census, as an essential pastoral tool, should be at the disposal of every parish staff. If it is not, it should be made so.[4]

Father Schuyler's census card has some additional features beyond the card cited above. Occupational level can be correlated between the members of the parish and the residents of the community as presented in the U. S. Bureau of the Census reports. Also, the rental value makes it possible to ascertain whether there is any discrepancy between the economic level of the members and that of the community in general. His card is shown on the following page,[5] (Figure 7).

Mobility studies reveal that on the average, about one out of five persons moves each year. This is why many large churches must receive over two hundred new members each year just to maintain the same steady total membership; any growth in size must be above this "replacement" group. Kloetzli and Hillman show this problem graphically in Figure 8.[6]

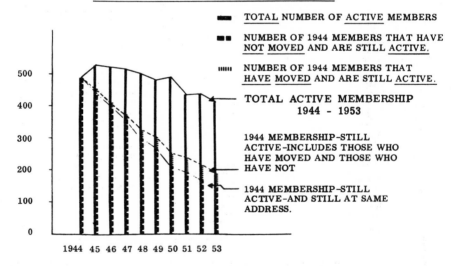

Figure 8.

[4] Joseph B. Schuyler, S. J., "Parish Census," *Catholic Management Journal*, Vol. 1, No. 2, Spring, 1958, p. 9.

[5] *Ibid.*, p. 7.

[6] Walter Kloetzli and Arthur Hillman, *Urban Church Planning* (Philadelphia: Muhlenberg Press, 1958), p. 126.

Many other characteristics could be listed here, and many more will come to the mind of the thoughtful pastor or church board—characteristics of the constituency that must be taken into account for intelligent planning and appropriate programing. We must now turn to the formal structure of this constituency as it is organized into a congregation.

ADMINISTRATION AND ORGANIZATION

A common complaint by parishioners is that some project or other is "the minister's idea." An influential charter member "had some pet idea and before we knew it, the whole thing was railroaded through the annual meeting." Projects begun with such suspicion and lack of general support are usually in for a long up-hill fight.

Is it possible to avoid such emotion-laden handicaps in church administration? Both the experience of numerous administrators and the principles of group dynamics point to less emotional and more objective foundations for any new venture. There is a better way to initiate change and begin new work than on the personal basis of "My idea's better than your idea" or "We did it this way in the last church I belonged to."

Too frequently, leaders try to provide answers to questions that the group has not raised, and solutions to problems that the members do not know exist. Unless people come to accept a proposition, they will not act upon it no matter how logically it is presented. On the other hand, when members of a group have participated in studying a situation and have become personally involved in discovering problems that exist in their midst, the motivation and energy that are released in providing a solution is often amazing.

Rather than jump to some conclusion about "what ought to be done" as typical hyper-active Americans are prone to do, let us begin by surveying the situation and objectively analyzing the needs. Then, when a program or plan of action is proposed to the whole congregation, "the facts speak for themselves" and "the evidence has shown that our church needs to do thus and so." The whole matter is taken out of the subjective, personally involved, emotionally clouded sphere, and the issues stand forth in clear focus on their own merit.

The same line of thinking ought to be followed in preparing a congregation to take this initial step of beginning a survey. If the parish survey "is the pastor's idea, some new gimmick he picked up at a summer workshop to get us to give more money or participate more, or *something . . . ,*" then the results of the survey will not interest the constituency nor effect administrative and organizational changes.

It is not safe to take for granted that everyone knows the way in which authority and responsibility are delegated by the constitution of the church. Frequently, a close look at church records reveals the fact that the constitution and by-laws have not been revised or brought up to date for several decades; meanwhile, the church has changed drastically in size, staff, and program.

The author once assigned twenty theological seminary field work students the task of constructing a table of organization of the local congregation to which each was assigned. In most cases this was the first complete table of organization that had been drawn up in the church's life and in many instances the channels of communication were not clearly defined.

It is not enough that everyone "means well," or that they are "always willing to help." Work must be delegated, reported on, and evaluated. Someone must be responsible and accountable for each task. The more clearly these administrative factors are defined, the less likelihood there is for confusion, hard feelings, overlapping, and oversights. Good administrative structure need not stifle spontaneity nor make the work of the church any less "spiritual"; nor does disorganization guarantee piety.

Responsibility should usually be more widely distributed than it is to prevent over-work of a faithful few. To secure a wider distribution of vitally interested and functionally involved members it is usually necessary to widen the base of democratic authority and responsibility. This can be accomplished by increasing the number on the governing board or council of the church as the membership grows. A clear line should be drawn between policy-making functions and the activities involved in executing these policies. Even if the same persons might sometimes do both, it is still necessary to keep the two clearly in mind. Too often policy is haphazardly evolved out of this or that which simply "is done" or "has *always* been done."

Obviously no one constitution or table of organization can suffice for every church since each congregation is unique in many details even while all have the same mission in the world. A sample table of organization appears in Figure 9. One should be drawn showing how things are organized at present. Another should be drawn showing an ideal structure—filling in gaps and eliminating duplication if such are noticed. Begin by listing every conceivable activity the church conducts or is involved in and then gradually group them under natural categories. Consult the "model constitution" and other organizational aids from denominational headquarters. Synodical, district, or diocesan leaders can provide broader perspective and are usually available to consult on such matters. Unfortunately, they are usually consulted only when there is "trouble."

Authority and *responsibility* are inextricably related, and should be uppermost in one's mind while the table of organization is being constructed. Many churches fear the term "authority," yet authority must rest *somewhere* with some person or group. It is better to be frank about

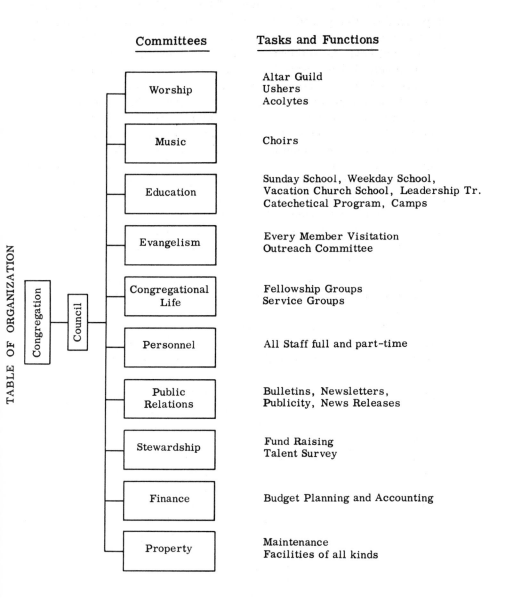

Figure 9.

this than to imply it indirectly, keep it a secret, or leave it to chance. The other side of the coin is responsibility. There can be no authority without responsibility. Every leader and worker must be held accountable. On the other hand, no one should be held accountable for any function that he does not have the authority to carry out. Lack of clarity at this point has frequently led to costly delays, hard feelings, and wasted effort.

Every task worth doing deserves a *"job description,"* including the limits of the assignment, *when* it is to be accomplished, and to whom a *report* about its completion should be made. Only then is it possible to *evaluate* the work done and plan appropriately for the future. *Selection* of workers, volunteers, nominees for office, and so forth, is made much simpler if there is such a clear idea of the task to be performed, the skills and abilities needed for the job, and the standards required. This is most obvious in the Christian Education program of the church, but is just as true in other areas. One church had three certified public accountants whose advice and suggestions were never sought in connection with budget and accounting problems in the church's fiscal structure. A sorely inadequate Sunday School teacher may linger on the staff for years simply because there are no objective standards or criteria by which an impartial evaluation can be made, and perhaps no clear policies of selection in the first place.

Planning and *co-ordination* constitute another pair of administrative functions that can facilitate the work of the church. A clear plan stating the objectives of the group and the procedures to be used in accomplishing the goal can improve motivation and morale. There is nothing more demoralizing than a feeling of purposelessness in the group, whether it be an auxiliary group of the church, or the congregation as a whole. With a specific, simple plan to guide the group, progress can be checked at various stages against the charted course. Proper co-ordination conserves energy and avoids overlapping. It makes the task of public relations easier because a clear goal and specific method are explained in a briefer space to members as well as to outsiders. Morale is improved whenever confusion is reduced and steady progress is realized toward an accepted and achievable goal. Most churches are quite successful in tangible projects such as erecting a building, or remodeling their present structures. It seems less obviously necessary to plan long range programs involving spiritual and social growth, and to co-ordinate interpersonal relationships and personal efforts.

One hesitates to pose an "ideal" pattern for all congregations in terms of structure. Here and there advice has been offered concerning the number of souls one pastor can care for, and the relationships within "institutional" churches where large staffs work in specialized areas. Another question concerns relationships between clergy and laity, between women's, men's, and youth's auxiliaries, and the congregation as a whole.

The most comprehensive statement with which the writer is familiar tries to sum up all the parts of the church and show their proper relationship and orientation.

> To proffer some sort of norm, we might say that the perfectly organized parish, in the most complete sense, is a functioning social system:
> of such size and physical equipment;
> such numerical proportions among priests, staff, lay leaders and other members;
> such a network of cooperating and mutually appreciated relationships and societies;
> so consciously possessed in its members of the knowledge of Christian doctrine and morals;
> so dedicated to the achievement of communal and personal holiness through use of Mass and Sacraments and pursuit of the two great laws of divine and fraternal love;
> so constant in its maintenance of the primacy of its spiritual values and apostolic commission over co-ordinated subsidiary temporal values;
> so welded by the communal concern of its members that there exists the practical and exploited opportunity for the spiritual and derivatively temporal richness of the faith to be brought to its every actual and potential member and to every institution of its coextensive civic community.[7]

That is surely a large order, but all administration and outward organization must be only a means to such a noble end. When organizational detail and administrative routine become ends in themselves in the church, surely this must be some form of socio-political idolatry. Then, indeed, it would be time again for self-examination and reformation.

LATENT AND MANIFEST PATTERNS [8]

Outlining a table of organization and creating charts of responsibility could be a real disservice if one believed naïvely that these correspond *exactly* to the facts of life. They are only rough estimates and goals to be striven toward. Ideals do not always correspond to reality.

Frequently we know the "power behind the throne" to be persons other than the duly elected officers or "stated" leaders. The "formal" leaders may not take decisive action until they have discovered the "sense of the meeting" or until the venerable old "patriarch" has spoken his

[7] Joseph B. Schuyler, S. J., "Potential Elements of Organization and Disorganization in the Parish as Seen in Northern Parish," *American Catholic Sociological Review,* Vol. 18, No. 2, June, 1957, p. 104.

[8] See Francis Stuart Chapin's *Contemporary American Institutions: A Sociological Analysis* (New York: Harper and Row, Inc., 1935).

mind and given his advice. As pastor of a congregation, the writer found it quite as essential to have an informal cup of coffee with a few informal leaders as to bring formal motions through the more clearly structured "Robert's Rules of Order." This was particularly true in initiating new projects such as the sponsorship of Displaced Persons. It would be quite unrealistic not to make allowance for these informal influences and "unofficial leaders" in any consideration of the structure of the congregation.

These latent forces and patterns of influence need not necessarily be considered bad or destructive; quite to the contrary they often represent the older members of the group with the longest history of experience and seasoned judgment. In any case they cannot be ignored. It is usually better to allow expression among these people than to try to suppress them by sheer force. In World War II the powerful German Army learned to take the "underground" as seriously as their uniformed enemies in the open lines of battle. The gnarled root structure of an old apple tree is just as important to the life of the tree as the beautiful leafy branches heavy with fruit.

Not until now have we been ready to discuss the strategy of the church to meet the needs of the people in a given community. It has been necessary to take a backward look at the origin and history of this particular church, to analyze the nature and situation of its membership, and to see how the church is put together both in formal organization and in intimate influences. Now we may proceed to the use of our collected data.

CHAPTER 5

THE STRATEGY
OF THE MISSION

The purpose of studying the community and analyzing the structure of the congregation cannot be idle curiosity, nor even good sociological research. It must serve to further the *mission* of the Church. This study is valuable in direct proportion to its usefulness in helping the church minister to more effectively relate the Gospel to man's present situation. Therefore, we need to ask what relevance all the statistics and survey data have for the strategy of the Church's mission.

Surprisingly enough, research proves just as beneficial in unexpected ways as in those ways for which it was originally intended. Inventors, such as Thomas Edison, have been hard on the trail of one problem only to discover an incidental bit of information, which itself became the big discovery. Occasionally this has turned into a new and profitable product for the company which had originally been concerned about another problem.

Strategic areas where this information will be useful are, among others, the following: reports to annual congregational meetings, reports to the denominational headquarters, answers to questions raised by the architect concerning remodeling or building plans, evangelism missions, public relations, budget planning, program planning, and evaluation of the program.

One of the most difficult tasks of an established group is to change its program to conform to new developments and needs. The "We've always done it this way" philosophy has a most rigidifying influence. Inertia seems to be as strong a force in social institutions as among physical objects. The longer a practice or program has been in operation the more obvious it appears to members of the group that this is not only the best way to do things, but the only way to do them. "But we've *never* paid an organist and choir director." "*Of course,* we run a dining concession at the State Fair; we couldn't *possibly* meet our budget any other way." "It's not any use trying _____ (fill in any activity you wish); nobody would come out for it anyway." "It just wouldn't seem like church any more if we didn't _____." "If he doesn't like things as they are, why doesn't he go join some other church?"

> The overworked and harassed priest, like the enthusiastic and energetic layman, tends to judge only from the surface of the parish. He sees the immediately visible and the easily measurable behavior of the parishioners. His natural optimism and loyalty to the Church may provide a state of mind in which it will never occur to him to question the obvious. . . .
>
> Even the most casual survey of the parish by a trained social scientist will bring to light objective facts which will dim this nimbus of optimism. It will open up areas of spiritual activity and suggest procedures through which large numbers of people may receive the benefits of religious ministrations. In other words, scientific social research uncovers not only the negative elements of the parochial system but also gives new insights into positive programs of improvement. Above all, it lifts the veil of illusion and permits the observer to judge critically and objectively.[1]

It would not be amiss to remind ourselves once more what the nature of the Church is and what its real mission is. There are those who believe that all it takes to make something "church work" is to do it within the four walls of a church. Churches have taken up the strangest projects; but if asked why a certain church was engaged in this or that particular activity, a sound rationale would be hard to find.

We need to go back and consider the "ecclesia," the people called by God to be reconciled to Him, to believe in Him so genuinely that they would worship Him alone, the people whose mission is, in turn, to call others into this reconciled and reconciling fellowship, the Kingdom of Heaven. Could this then be the criterion? That the church should try to use as many methods and opportunities as possible to implement worship of God, loving service to mankind, and spiritual growth in grace among the individuals of the household of faith? Would not this con-

---

[1] Joseph H. Fichter, S. J., *Social Relations in the Urban Parish* (Chicago: The University of Chicago Press, 1954), pp. 242-43. (Copyright 1954 by The University of Chicago.)

form to Christ's summation of the law? Love of God above all things (worship), love of neighbor (service), and love of self (growth). This does not mean that the formally organized Church is the only agency through which these things can be done; but somehow, what the Church does must be shown to be a necessary, or at least indirect, contribution to these ends. The fact that the Church cannot provide *all* services and produce *all* growth means that the Church must be selective and choose those means whereby its resources can make the greatest impact.

The writer is so convinced that the Church should throw most of its energies into two of its unique functions: the Sacraments of Baptism and Holy Communion, and the special ministries to the crises of life such as marriage and death, that an entire section is set aside (Part Two) for their consideration. Worship is obviously a generic part of all these services. Nevertheless, the church, as a social institution, and as a dynamic confluence of group interactions, becomes involved in many activities only indirectly related to the specific services mentioned above.

PARTICIPATION PATTERNS IN PARISH LIFE

The suggested census card (page 60) proposes two categories of participation: the activities or groups a person is now involved in, and the activities or services a person is willing to volunteer for. It is important that we ascertain what is involved in these participation patterns. Since the year of a member's birth and the year that member joined the church are both listed, it is possible to discover whether membership in groups such as choir, women's groups, etc., cover an adequate sampling of the congregation, both as to age and length of membership. For example, are newer members being assimilated into the congregational life of the parish; are certain age groups not attracted to the choir or included in the staff of the Sunday School; or is there a great deal of overlapping among a relatively small group of over-active members? These questions begin to arise as patterns in the statistics appear. The implications are often quite simple. Perhaps the organization of another group (e.g., a youth choir, a tea for new women members, etc.) or activity might make participation more congenial to some who are not now interested.

If the church is located in a lodging house or residential hotel section of the city (*see* Figure 5), perhaps the survey will reveal many single persons or widowed people not living in family units, but in isolation. There may not be any groups at present in which these people find natural and comfortable participation, especially if the church stresses work with children and aims for the "normal" family groupings. They may feel left out or out of place, teased as "spinsters and bachelors," and not accepted as they are. Strategy and program planning should suggest themselves from these findings.

It is not necessary to belabor the point nor show all the possible cross correlations, but it might be suggestive to illustrate how the age-sex pyramid, participation, and community resources were all related in the case of the Holy Trinity study. One result of the two maps shown on the following pages was the organization of a regular group for older people within the church's program (Figures 10 and 11). In the membership, 7 per cent were 65 years of age and over, whereas, in the community, about 9-10 per cent were within that age bracket (within the census tract of the church the percentage was between 10 and 12). See map in Figure 9. Couple this with the reduced map (Figure 11) which shows that there are no organized groups for the aged as such in the area; and it becomes apparent that there is a large cause waiting to be served. These can meet during the day when the building is relatively empty. Older persons should help plan it. The trend is toward an increased group of aged.

Sorting out the stewardship participation of the members by age categories can aid in long-range planning because it is significant from which decades (those in their forties, fifties, sixties, etc.) the major proportion of support is coming. What guarantee does the church have that the younger generation will replace the older generation in financial support ten or twenty years from now? The following graphs indicate three ways of dissecting these data and are self-explanatory (Figure 12).[2] Two are age-sex pyramids.

A large number of laymen, Deacons, Stewards, or District Captains (with sub team captains in each district) could share in the pastoral care oversight of the needs of the members. In a large church perhaps one such worker for every fifty members in a given area could assist the council or board in their task as pledged to in their installation. One such typical installation service reads as follows:

> To assist the Pastor in the care of the sick and needy, in the cultivation of harmony among the members, in the promotion of the general welfare of the Congregation, and in the furtherance of Christ's Kingdom, at home and abroad.[3]

Distribution of such responsible laymen could be guided by the membership distribution as recorded geographically on the dot map. This so-

---

[2] "Harron and North Methodist Churches, Northwest Minneapolis and Vicinity, Spring, 1959," A Study by the Bureau of Social and Religious Research, Murray H. Leiffer, Director, Alan Waltz, Chief Research Assistant, Garrett Biblical Institute, Evanston, Illinois.

[3] *Common Service Book of the Lutheran Church* (Philadelphia: The Board of Publication of the United Lutheran Church, 1917), p. 288.

PER-CENT OF POPULATION 1950 65 AND OVER

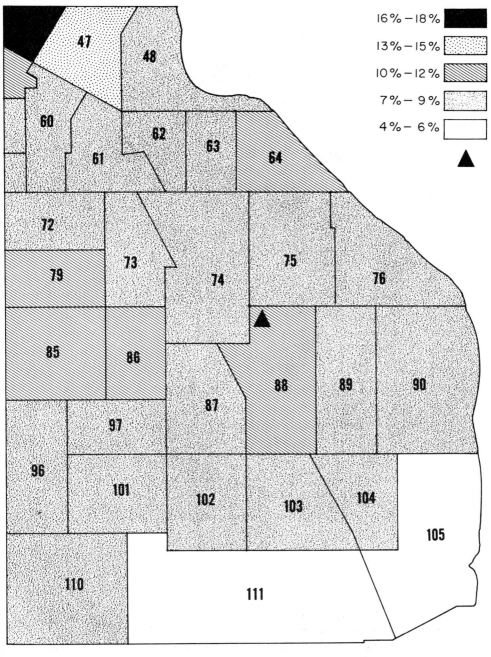

16% – 18%
13% – 15%
10% – 12%
7% – 9%
4% – 6%

Figure 10.

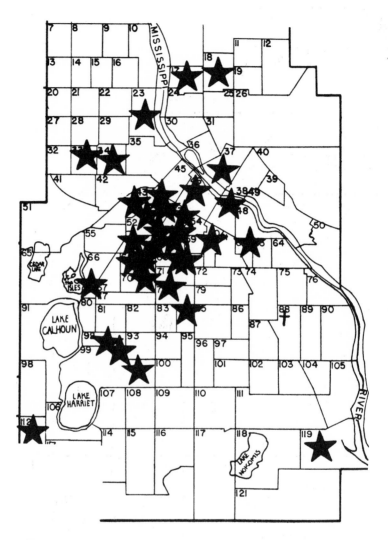

Figure 11. Recreation for older people and distribution of organized groups. Community Welfare Council, Hennepin County, Minnesota, 1955.

called "Shepherding Plan" has worked effectively in many parishes. It is a systematic and personal way to keep track of the needs of the members in cases of childbirth, illness, death, hardship of one kind or another, as well as the happy occasions such as anniversaries.

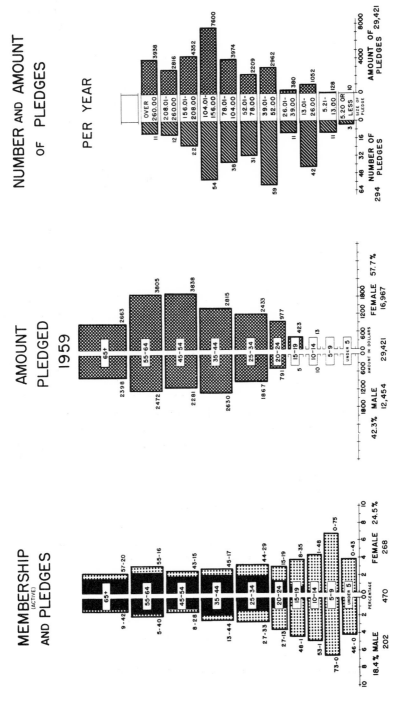

Figure 12.

Above all, let us not have participation merely for participation's sake. Sheer, brute loyalty, merely attending one meeting after another so there will be a good "turn out," is hardly noble enough reason for participation. It is perfectly possible that one or another auxiliary organization of the church ought to fold up if it fulfills no real *need.* To keep it alive year after year by artificial respiration is no kindness to anyone and no great service to the Kingdom. Let it die in peace. If it should turn out that a terrible void is felt in the lives of many people, it can be filled.

Let us not forget that there are many people for whom active, extrovert participation in groups is too threatening; and there are others, whose *needs* are adequately met through other means. Also there are many levels: active participation, passive participation, active observation, passive observation, active dissenters, passive dissenters, and isolationists. Try to push an isolationist into active church participation, and you may lose him from the church permanently. Would it not have been better to have let him come at his own level, perhaps quietly slipping into the back seat of the balcony, and (as in one case the writer observed) slipping out just before the Benediction because he couldn't stand the handshaking and the "How are you this morning." He was too honest to say, "Fine," and too ashamed to say how he really felt. Some cases should be reserved for personal pastoral care and not subjected to group participation, at least until such time as they have grown and matured to the minimum demands of group experience.

There may be some real theological confusion at this point. There are three Greek words translated in English as love." Ἔρως (*eros*) connotes sexual attraction; φίλος (*philos*) refers to friendship or comradeship as in the Latin *socius,* which includes social relations; and, ἀγάπη (*agape*) in the New Testament is reserved for the love of God, unmerited grace, redeeming love, yes, even love for one's enemies. Now, the Christian is to express the love of God, the sense that all manner of men are greatly valued in the sight of God, toward his fellows. But this does not mean he has the same social relationships with everyone. A college lad relates one way toward his classmates, another way toward his roommate in "bull sessions," and still another way toward his girl friend at a party. He is not being "unChristian in thus discriminating between these people, all of whom he may "like" within the range of *philos* or friendship.

Fellowship is a wonderfully enriching experience, but it is just possible that this has been over-emphasized sometimes as a mark of the Church. Perhaps that is why our Protestant denominations are so stratified along class and socio-economic levels. This might also account for why the Roman Catholic Church has much better out-reach across social class barriers and at least as good a record in racial relations. One can be a good member if he *only* worships God through the Mass and receives Communion, regardless of whether he "joins" various guilds and sodalities. Belonging to the same parish does not necessitate (nor, of course, does it preclude) the "You-invite-me-to-your-birthday-party-and-I'll-invite-you-to-mine" type of social fellowship. This has been the problem when women's groups have taken turns meeting in each other's homes, and, all of a sudden, it dawns on one of the women from a very inadequate house across the tracks that she really is not as much a part of this group as she had thought. She cannot possibly take her turn as hostess, and so quietly drops out of the picture. The same pertains to the other marks of natural social attraction—similar clothing, education, manners, interests, abilities, etc. If these are to be also marks of identification in church membership, we will have to continue to split our denominations into class and status groups as well as ethnic, racial, and other special *philos* loyalties.

CHRISTIAN EDUCATION

More surveys have been made of the parish education aspect of the Church's program than any other phase of the Church's work for two reasons: denominational boards of Christian Education have suggested it, and, secondly, the fairly complete statistics are already available from the Sunday School secretary's records, which frequently include rather detailed registration forms.

A sample of the card (Figure 13) used at Holy Trinity, together with excerpts from the letter the Director of Christian Education sent to each Sunday School teacher in advance of the survey are exhibited below.

> One part of this study concerns a survey of our Sunday School. . . .
> On this card you will obtain certain information about your children.
> These cards will be used primarily as research cards, but also for permanent records in our Sunday School. . . . If you cannot obtain all of the information from your children, we ask that you call their parents. We are sure that if you explain this survey to your children and their parents in a relaxed and kind way they will accept it readily and be glad to help you in obtaining this information.

The same suggestions about cross-correlating the data from the card explained on pp. 71-72 also apply to this parish education card. The machinery for gathering the facts are already organized through teachers and departmental leaders.

Naturally, any Sunday School data must be supplemented by Vacation Church School, Weekday Church School, and any other parish educa-

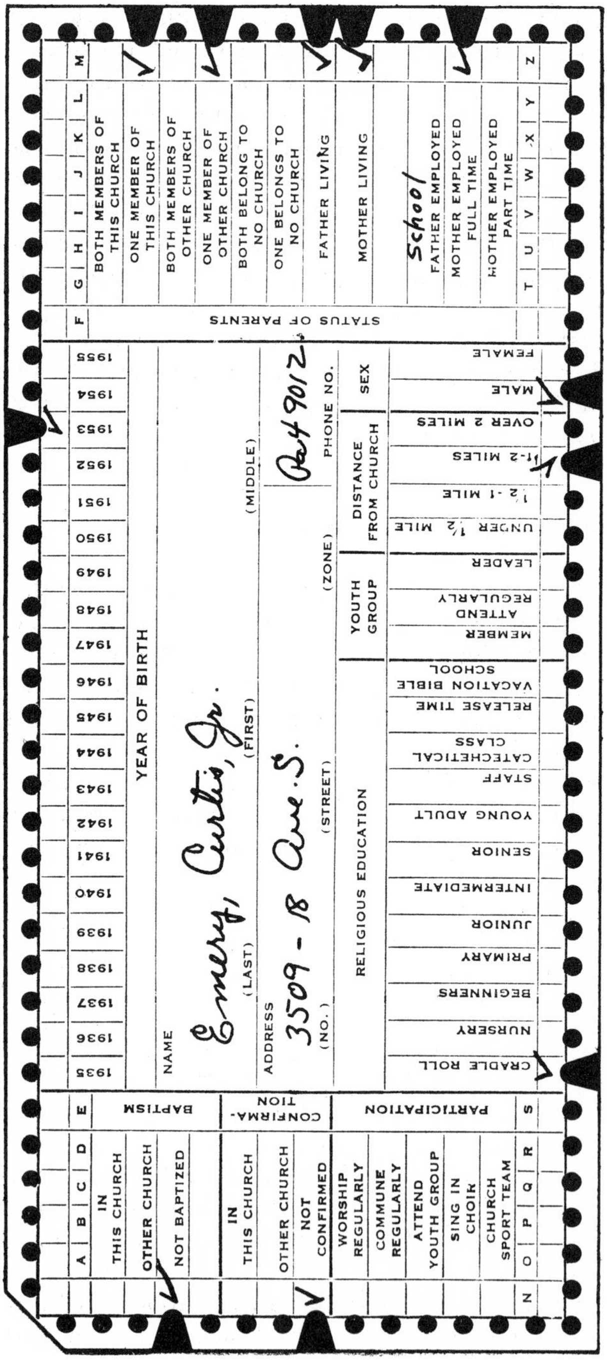

Figure 13. Parish Education Card.

tion program statistics. Also, the entire roll of child members must be checked against this list.

Charts can sometimes show at a glance any unusual population patterns that suggest increase or decrease in certain class or departmental enrollments. On the same chart can be plotted the ratio between the church's coverage of given age groups in relation to the number of children in the same age groups according to the school district lists or other census tabulations that pertain to the community of which the church is a part. Allowances must be made for ethnic and religious representation in the community. For example, a minority Protestant church might be located in a predominantly Roman Catholic neighborhood. Nevertheless, the comparisons can be illuminating. On the graph following (Figure 14), the elementary school list figures (for the seven

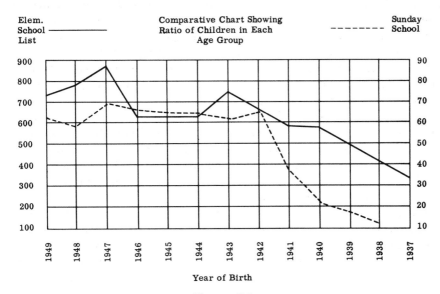

Figure 14.

schools serving the area Holy Trinity considered its community) are shown in hundreds, the Sunday School enrollments are shown in tens, and the two lines are superimposed in overlapping fashion. The birth rate is clearly evident, being lower in the depression years of the thirties and reaching a high point in 1949. Note the sudden drop in participation after confirmation age (about 14 years of age; i.e., those born in 1942).

It is important to encompass the whole range of Christian Education activities and not confine the study to the Sunday School and one or two other obvious programs. There may be a released time program in co-operation with other churches, summer camp programs, catechetical classes for the young, and adult membership instruction for persons joining the church, leadership training, and other regular educational activities.

Other, less obvious, aspects of the educational ministry of the church might include phases of the youth work, women's groups, couples' club, men's groups, altar guild, choir, etc. The reason for making this list as comprehensive as possible is that an over-view of the total educational program can be seen. Only in this way can overlapping be spotted, economical use of audio-visual aids and other resources be determined, and a continuing on-going curriculum be planned. Usually the denominational board of Christian education has arranged a systematic and carefully graded series of materials for the Sunday School and youth groups. If these are followed, the major areas of Bible knowledge and the important themes of doctrine and church history will be covered over a number of years. These materials are becoming more and more functional and relevant to daily life as highly trained religious education specialists have been added to these denominational staffs.

It is in the less highly organized and sometimes independent adult groups that co-ordination tends to break down and a program of unrelated topics such as "the local basketball coach," "flower arranging," "Mr. Blank's pictures from his recent duck hunting trip," and "a speaker to be announced" grow like Topsy. For adult members who attend these meetings year in and year out the picture is often confusing and mostly remembered for highs and lows of enthusiasm and disappointment. It hardly contributes to one of the three aims we set forth earlier as the legitimate mission of the Church.

What is the prescribed responsibility for all this range of educational opportunity as far as the Committee on Christian education of the local congregation is concerned? Now might be a good time to make a comprehensive list of objectives and areas that need to be covered and to relate them to specific programs. Many of the gaps in the Christian education of the congregation can well be filled through already existing groups and organizations. Perhaps novel methods will suggest themselves as in the case of the church where fifty or sixty interested adults used their class period to discuss the sermon with the preacher in what they called a "Talk Back" session. Unless some committee or supervisory person is responsible for taking this comprehensive over-view, the educational work of the church is left to dozens of unrelated groups, "program chairmen," and teachers all working along conscientiously but in isolation and perhaps even at cross purposes.

Christian education is also related to many other divisions of the Church's ministry such as evangelism, stewardship, and perhaps all the other committees on the Table of Organization (*see* Figure 9).

UNFILLED NEEDS AND CHRISTIAN SERVICE

One of the most futile of all efforts is to try to arouse enthusiasm in some group for a "project," just for the sake of having a project—to have *something* to do. Perhaps this accounts for the short life and failure of so many church projects. There has been no motivation because the project seemed artificial. John Dewey created quite a stir when he proposed that the best place to begin was with the "awareness of a problem," or, as it has sometimes been called, "a felt need."

If the findings of a study on the setting, structure, and strategy of a church have been thoroughly interpreted to the constituency, there will surely appear things that need doing urgently. Three sheets should be drawn up with the following headings: (1) findings concerning the community in order of their significance; (2) findings concerning the life and structure of the congregation listed in order of their importance; and, (3) findings concerning the program or strategy of the church, listed according to their priority or urgency.

Needs may range from welfare problems of certain families or aged persons, to better preparation for marriage on the part of engaged couples in the church. There might be the problem of integrating new members, minority groups, alcoholic or emotionally disturbed persons into the fellowship of the church.

The most pressing need of one church might be to hold the youth after confirmation while another needs to meet the problem of a mobile population as its worthy challenge. All these unfulfilled needs should not be dealt with in general; they must be singled out and dealt with in specific. It is much better for the morale and spiritual life of the members to implement some program in a particular area than to feel deeply moved about generalities with which they feel impotent to deal. "Be ye doers of the word and not hearers only."

We cannot call it Christian service if we limit our emphasis to "study groups" about the "great problems of our day." Such concern must be translated into *action* in terms of specific needs that have name and address. But we need not choose between theory and practice. Having become aware of "the burdensome problem of the aged," members must now make calls on old Anna Smith at the home for the aged and on John Doe upstate at the mental hospital. They must do something specific for the patients in the nursing home two blocks down the street from the church.

These are not "projects" that have to be thought up in a denominational headquarters or literature committee (although they have their place in the larger issues of world relief, resettlement of displaced persons, church sponsored adoption agencies, and social action); they can grow naturally and inevitably from a good look at our community and church.

THE EXPEDITORS: PAID STAFF AND VOLUNTEER WORKERS

There is nothing so obvious about a task as that it has to be done by *someone* and that it has to be done in *some way* and at *some time*. Add a couple other factors and a "job description" soon develops.

Industry and business in general are discovering the absolute necessity of the job description. Unless a person knows what is expected of him, what the requirements and the limits of his duties are, he can hardly be blamed for not fulfilling his assignment satisfactorily. Students are quick to point out to a teacher that he has not made the assignment clear and that, therefore, they shouldn't have to be tested on that material at this time. Sometimes a worker, perhaps the janitor, is driven in desperation to ask for a job description only after considerable conflict and hard feelings have developed.

With the increasing number of churches using a multiple or staff ministry, the need for defining the roles of the various workers is becoming more evident. While making a survey of the role of parish worker, the author discovered a tremendous variety in the definition of the task; and the most frequent complaint among the parish workers questioned was the uncertainty about what was and what was not their responsibility. Another bothersome problem was the lack of clarity concerning to whom they were responsible. One replied, "I'm responsible to no one; I just do what I think needs to be done." Amazingly, this frequently works; but as often as not, it accounts in part for the short tenure of many church workers who can no longer stand the frustration and move on for a fresh start.

Sometimes we recognize the need for defining the role of paid staff— organist, choir director, janitor, office secretary, etc.; but we fail to define the task of the volunteer—the Sunday School superintendent, officers and teachers, youth advisors, church council members, Deacons, etc. Consequently, they have no real yardstick by which to judge whether they succeeded or failed in their work. Again, it is neither good for morale nor really fair to leave any worker in this uncertain position.

Job descriptions need not be rigid and fixed for all time. They should be modified and changed as the situation and need vary. Perhaps it will become evident that two persons should be asked to do the work that formerly (perhaps when the church membership was smaller) could easily be handled by one.

Who are the volunteers and active leaders? By sorting out these categories, one can see if they represent a cross-section of the church or a narrow group of old established stand-bys. If the volunteers are offered guidance, direction, and some appreciation, it may be possible to broaden the base of leadership and volunteer participation. This has proven especially true in teacher training programs in parish education.

PUBLIC RELATIONS AND RELIGIOUS REPORTING

Good public relations begin from within. It is important that the members of the church understand the mission and program of the Church before they attempt to interpret it to outsiders. One cannot take anything for granted at this point. Just because the pastor and some church council members see a given problem does not mean the main body of the membership have come to the same conclusion—even if they have all been exposed to the same facts and figures. Some folks are suspicious of figures and will reply, "Maybe figures don't lie, but liars can figure." A majority of the people have not been trained in scientific or logical thinking.

In order that the parishioners understand the rationale of any program (e.g., the findings from this survey), it is necessary to present the facts in clear and simple form. Perhaps one phase at a time can be included each month with the regular monthly bulletin or newsletter presenting the graphs, charts, maps, or statistics to make that segment of the proposal clear. The crucial facts and interpretations can be presented as a whole report in mimeographed or printed form in conjunction with the stewardship effort, the annual meeting of the congregation, or any other time when the work of the whole church is being presented.

A self-study may reveal a need for better communication with other churches, community agencies, denominational headquarters, and so forth. In this sense, public relations is far wider in scope than mere publicity, although appropriate publicity can contribute to good public relations. Mass media of communication should not be overlooked, and each medium has its special usefulness for certain purposes, such as newspaper, radio, TV, outdoor advertising, handbills, and direct mail.

Strategic times to inform the community and wider public about the present and proposed work of the church will vary from one place to another. Considerable curiosity can be aroused in the neighborhood about a church which is for the first time taking that neighborhood seriously and trying conscientiously to serve the people. Timing is important. There is no reason why several news stories highlighting different aspects of a survey cannot be released over a period of months. Good interpretative pictures will appeal to news editors and religious editors if they are imaginatively original and avoid the old stereotypes of hand-shaking, groundbreaking, mortgage burning, or a line-up pose with no action or self-evident message.

If there is no policy, budgeted allotment, or plan for assuring good and continuous public relations, the Church is missing an opportunity to strengthen the strategy of its mission.

CONTINUING EVALUATION

Living organisms are not static—that would be a contradiction in terms. We go to our doctor or dentist for a periodic check-up because the condition of our health is constantly changing. So, a self-study will be outmoded in a fairly short time, and like an old X-ray will be valuable chiefly for purposes of comparison, to check trends and trace new developments.

Certain aspects of the community may not need to be checked more than every five years, and the massive U. S. Census Bureau reports make good reading only every ten years. Other aspects, e.g., concerning the constituency of the congregation and the Sunday School, need an annual evaluation. The budget, the programs of the auxiliary organizations, and the Christian Education programs are planned usually in annual cycles at least.

Comparisons cannot be made from year to year unless the same categories are used and items in those categories are defined in the same terms consistently. A twenty-five or fifty year membership graph is not reliable if the dips in the line represent years "we cleaned out the dead wood" and the years in between represent inflationary figures. It is useful to define what is meant by an "active" member and to distinguish between baptized, confirmed, and communing members. Will there be a category for "inactive" or "non-resident" members? Without clarification and consistency, any comparison from year to year can be very misleading.

If the same forms or methods of gathering the census of the membership can be routinely integrated with other functions, it need not be burdensome. In the currently popular "Every Member Visitation," the machinery for a canvass is already in operation, the secretarial tasks of typing members' names onto cards, the mailings, the system of tabulations and record keeping are usually working smoothly and routinely. Merely asking a few extra questions at the time of the stewardship solicitations or having a few extra items to check off on a survey card will be easier than organizing an entirely new campaign for gathering the parish census data.

Only a continuing evaluation will show the members of the church that the initial study was undertaken seriously. Otherwise, what is the point of gathering a lot of information? One must check and see whether the changes made in the program, the new approaches and methods initiated as a result of the survey, were justified and adequate to meet the needs they were intended to care for.

There is here the opportunity to distribute the responsibility for the annual survey among the members so that over the years a large percentage of the membership will be intimately informed and "on their toes" concerning the *setting* of the parish, the *structure* of the congregation, and the *strategy* of the mission. This could result in not one minister or a few leaders dragging along a reluctant and complacent multitude, but, rather, all the members as part of one and the same Body of Christ, the Church, working eagerly for the same goal: (1) the worship of God, (2) the service of mankind, and (3) growth in grace.

The work of the local church is rich in the complexity of its challenge and the blessings of its service; but, we must lift our eyes to the horizon where we see the Church extending far beyond the confines of the parish boundaries, far beyond this little community measured in a few square miles, and far beyond the needs of the few called into this little fellowship. We must turn now to the Church-at-Large.

CHAPTER 6

THE CHURCH
UNIVERSAL

Too often pastors allow themselves to become swallowed up in the daily round; they forget that the whole is greater than any of its parts, and they act as if the Church Universal were confined within the periphery of their parishes. This is a fundamental mistake, with serious consequences. The Universal Church, as the embodiment of Christ in the world, must occupy first place in a pastor's religious purview. To this end, he should not only himself keep abreast of all world-wide Church movements but in addition he should so train his people.[1]

DENOMINATIONAL HERITAGE AND STRUCTURE

Jung was cited previously (page 22) concerning the importance of acknowledging one's heritage as a vital part of one's present personality structure. Some timid people think that repressing the fact that they are of Italian Catholic, German Lutheran, or Swedish Baptist background will somehow make them appear more cosmopolitan, broadminded, or even more "ecumenical." Yet, the fact remains that any Christian has become so within the context of some particular tradition. His Baptism is recorded in the book of a given parish church where later he learned about God, the Bible, and the Church, through Episcopal, Methodist, Presbyterian, or Lutheran Sunday School literature. We are simply affirming that the Universal Church has found expression in a variety of very specific and distinctive traditions.

Even the considerably *free* churches of the Congregational heritage have found it useful and necessary to band together for administrative, educational, and missionary effectiveness. The establishment of theo-

---

[1] Holland, *Op. cit.*, p. 16. Whereas this admonition would appear obvious as a charge to Protestant clergy; it is here given by an old, experienced priest to his brethren in the Roman Catholic Church.

logical seminaries, church colleges, homes for the aged and orphans, publishing houses for the dissemination of religious literature, summer camps, and the like, demonstrate the functional nature of denominationalism. One has the feeling that if a thousand completely autonomous and independent congregations were established in a remote area, they would soon begin to group themselves into larger and larger working associations. So much for a functional explanation.

The historical approach points to other reasons for denominationalism. The vast majority of churches have been deliberately established as missions by some church or group of churches (as represented by a synod or diocese) and, therefore, inevitably bear the stamp of tradition and structure that the founding fathers thought best. No matter how it changes its color and shape later in life, any local congregation owes much to its parent body, much as an individual is mightily influenced by his parents through the processes of heredity. Even in suburbia one will hear such a remark as this: "They call it The _____ Community Church, but it's really Baptist." Most denominations have exerted enough influences so that even councils of Protestant churches have not established more than a handful of so-called "non-denominational" or "interdenominational" congregations. And even where such has been the case, one or another minister has given it more of one denominational flavor than another. This is also seen in the military chaplaincy to some extent. "You don't usually use both grape juice and wine in Communion; you use one or the other," spells denominationalism.

In a seminary convocation address,[2] T. A. Kantonen stated the conviction that plurality began when the Church began, because cultural factors have always been present as part of God's providence and creation. At any rate, whatever diversity has developed in the Universal Church, it is sure to be perpetuated, or, at the very least be influential, in the individual congregations established.

Sometimes congregations are established by large, downtown "mother" churches as missions among their outlying membership; at other times they are established as financially dependent missions. In any case, a local congregation should sense its real dependence on Mother Church (call it synod, diocese, national headquarters, or what you will) as well as on sibling or sister churches within its denomination. This is not only in keeping with the spirit of Saint Paul as he tried to establish relations of mutual helpfulness and esteem among the early congregations, but it is exceedingly practical as well. Many are the congregations that became unnecessarily involved in problems because they did not "go through proper channels" in calling a pastor, or make use of the consulta-

---

[2] A lecture entitled "The Church as the Communion of Saints" given at the Northwestern Lutheran Theological Seminary Convocation in January, 1956, Minneapolis.

tion of experienced and mature church leaders in the denominational headquarters concerning the discipline or removal of an "impossible" pastor. This unfortunate situation often comes to pass because of a spirit within a congregation that they are sufficient unto themselves and must prove their strength and independence. The same unfortunate condition prevails when a church will refuse to go along with some enterprise which the majority of the delegates at convention have agreed upon. One senses here an adolescent immaturity, a rebellion against Mother, and maybe Father too.

Very few Protestants would be willing to take a "vow of obedience" such as a monk takes; but, no matter what name or form it has, the necessity of coming to grips with the problem of authority is a genuine problem that must be resolved. This can vary from co-operating with one's Bishop's causes in the more authoritarian structures, to supporting the general work voted on by the majority after the President or Moderator has called for a vote in a democratic assembly. "But," someone will say, "what about freedom of conscience and individual integrity?" Often this is rationalization. It is so easy to confuse laziness, stubbornness, inertia, and temper tantrums, with matters of "principle" and one's "rights." This could well be symptomatic of the maturity of a local congregation: its attitude toward, and relationships with, the Church as a denomination, and the sister churches that constitute it.

A mature church council and minister will not hesitate or regret to give a letter of transfer for one of the congregation's members to join another church in a neighborhood to which this person is moving. They will recognize that the strength of the army is not diminished if a soldier is transferred from one company to another. But this could logically lead to the next question: What if you transfer the soldier from one battalion to another? Has the army lost out in numerical strength then? This leads us to the question of attitudes toward other denominations of the evangelical tradition.

ECUMENICAL FELLOWSHIP AND CO-OPERATION [3]

Every true believer in Jesus Christ is a member of the Christian Church —the one, holy, catholic, and apostolic church. . . . The Christian Church is larger than any and all church organizations. It is the communion of all God's saints, of all God's redeemed children. . . . There must, therefore, be no narrow parochialism, no narrow denominationalism, no sectarianism, no selfishness, no unbrotherliness. . . . It will be

---

[3] *See* Keith Bridston's article, "The Cosmos and the Ego," *Religion in Life,* Vol. 28, No. 1, Winter, 1958-59, pp. 34-44, for an excellent application of ecumenicity to the theological education scene.

interested and concerned; it will be understanding and sympathetic; it will be contributive and co-operative. For the congregation will never forget that it is the church universal coming to form and expression in a given place. It will have an ecumenical spirit and outlook—always.[4]

There are a great many things that Christian churches can do better together than separately as individual denominations. Public officials are almost driven to distraction when they try to be fair in dealing with dozens of well meaning but hopelessly over-lapping church sponsored welfare projects. A superintendent of the large city hospital finds it much easier to deal with a unified program of pastoral care for Protestant patients under the guidance of one well qualified and trained hospital chaplain. The same is true of the city workhouse, jail, and court, of the state mental hospitals, and schools for mentally retarded. The public school administrator is much more co-operative if he is reasonably assured that all the squabbling and haggling for special privilege has been obviated by inter-denominational agreement and co-ordinated effort in a unified "release time program" of religious education. Here is the field for ecumenical co-operation through a local "council of churches."

At the University of Minnesota Hospital, a group of eight Protestant visiting chaplains, all ministers of local Minneapolis congregations, make regular pastoral calls on Protestant patients who might not otherwise be ministered unto because many of them come from a great distance. This program is under the auspices of the Greater Minneapolis Council of Churches. At the end of the year, a letter is sent to the official board of the congregation served by each visiting chaplain thanking that congregation for including the needs of these patients in its regular ministry. The purpose is twofold: first, simple appreciation; second, an attempt to interpret to the local congregation that this ministry is just as much a part of the chaplains' normal responsibility as is ministering to their own members. It matters little that one of these patients belongs to a church two hundred miles away, and perhaps to another denomination. And their pastor is not doing *extra*-curricular work nor taking *time off* from his regular church work in ministering unto them. Both the churches and the ministers involved have participated in practical ecumenicity.

Perhaps the largest area of co-operation is in the field of "released time" religious education, sometimes involving over half of the council of churches' budget. There are the audio-visual aids, rental libraries, leadership training institutes, religious census taking, social action work, ministries to the American Indian migrants in large urban centers, ministries to migrant workers, mass communications media such as radio

[4] Paul J. Hoh, *Parish Practice* (Philadelphia: Muhlenberg Press, 1944), pp. 165-66.

and television, and numerous other large areas of service in which the lone congregation, or even the few churches of this or that denomination, would not make a large enough impact. These are all typical and suitable areas for ecumenical co-operation.

There is no need for each denomination timidly and half-ashamedly to give up its unique distinctiveness in such ecumenical fellowship and service. One enjoys the rainbow because the colors retain their separate identity while at the same time blending their essence into a harmonious pattern. Quite the contrary is true of a box of watercolors in which the various brilliant colors have run together into a dirty and indistinguishable mess.

True fellowship does not consist in hiding one's true identity for fear of the possible conflicts or issues that the confrontation of true selves might produce. True fellowship is only possible with the acceptance of one another's unique attributes, and appreciation of one another's contributions. Nor does this have to result finally in agreement. Although the author cannot recall the source, it seems there is a motto that goes something like this: "Agree to differ, and resolve to love."

This principle put into practical terms can be illustrated in the worship services that are sometimes used by mixed groups, especially interdenominational youth meetings and camp meetings. Not infrequently, the feeling prevails that to make this service of worship "ecumenical," it should include a dash of this and a dab of that from quite a wide range of traditions. What results is not unlike the watercolors that have run together in the bottom of the box. Would it not be more true to the ecumenical spirit of sharing to use whatever forms are indigenous to the host church? If the meeting is in a Lutheran church, use the Matins or Vespers of the *Service Book and Hymnal;* if the service is in an Episcopal Church, use the *Book of Common Prayer;* in a Methodist church, use the *Methodist Hymnal* with whatever forms and rubrics belong to the Methodist discipline. In any case, let the particular tradition shine forth to its best advantage not only for the inspiration but the education of those to whom this way is strange. Thus can members of the various denominations grow in understanding and appreciation of each other's contributions. If, in the process, one takes sharp issue with his brother of another tradition, there is no harm done, if it's done in love. Perhaps some deep thinking, theological and practical re-evaluation, and soul-searching might profit both parties. Ecumenical fellowship and co-operation have led many, including the author, to deeper understanding and broader appreciation not only of other traditions but of one's own heritage. Thus one grows in the Church Universal. In the words of the Nicene Creed: "I believe one holy Catholic and Apostolic Church."

WORLD WIDE MISSION

Since Wendell Willkie's *One World*, since the United Nations, and since world travel has become commonplace, the common man has gradually learned to become almost as concerned about what happens in Formosa as on Main Street, as interested in the marriage of the Emperor's son in Japan as in the romance of a favorite Hollywood actress, as concerned about economic welfare in West Berlin as in the employment-unemployment ratio of his own home town. Has this world-view affected the church member as he compares the work of his local congregation with the progress and condition of the sister churches in distant parts of the world?

Anyone having the following experience of Professor Keene could not help but meditate on its significance as he did.

> Arriving early to speak before members of the Ahmadiyya Movement in Islam at their Washington, D.C., center, I was in time to witness the acceptance into membership in Islam of half a dozen persons, white and Negro. The ceremony was simple but to me profoundly significant, for there I saw Christians giving up their faith to become members of a different religion. This picture is being repeated across the country as six Ahmadiyya centers are now busily engaged in making converts to this Pakistani sect. Further, everyone knows persons who have studied books on theosophy, Vedanta, Zen Buddhism, Taoism—books whose religious roots are laid in Far Eastern religions—and have been deeply influenced by this study.[5]

Today one reads in church periodicals of rather ordinary clergymen from average churches returning from a month or more of world travel. They tell their congregations from first-hand observation of the progress that is being made on the mission fields supported by their denominational agencies. They report on how physical and spiritual ministries are being carried out in their name among the Arabs in concentration (or displaced persons) camps, or among the people in Hong Kong. Many congregations receive regular letters and reports from missionaries that they "sponsor," or for whom they pay a certain percentage of total support. In these ways the local congregation and the far-flung mission outpost sense their common enterprise as co-workers in the Universal Church.

Another attempt to broaden the outlook of the local parish is to refer to churches in foreign, and frequently underdeveloped, countries such as

---

[5] J. Calvin Keene, "Christianity's New Challenge and Opportunity," *Religion in Life,* Vol. 27, No. 3, Summer, 1958, p. 393.

Madagascar and Sumatra, as "younger churches," not as "foreign missions." Many Christians in old established churches and in countries where the Faith has been known and believed for hundreds of years, have come to look upon these younger sister churches with real inspiration and respect. They have seen in these new converts a willingness to sacrifice and witness, a joy in being born anew, that has made an older brother, who was born into the church and has ever since taken it for granted, stop and examine his own religious experience.

The world-wide mission of the Church Universal is clearly summed up in the Great Commission of Christ:

> All authority in heaven and on earth has been given to me. Go therefore and make disciples of all nations, baptizing them in the name of the Father and of the Son and of the Holy Spirit, teaching them to observe all that I have commanded you; and lo, I am with you always, to the close of the age.[6]

Just as it was necessary to consider the prime work of worship before discussing the "program" of the local congregation, so it is necessary to set the time and space perspective of the Universal Church before our eyes as the proper context of the congregation. This should be done deliberately and periodically to offset the hyper-active involvement in petty details. Only as the local congregation possesses this perspective can its life be truly integrated to the fullest in the Kingdom of God on earth. And only as the Church Militant is seen in relation to the Church Triumphant can the believer know his place and his destiny. We close this discussion of The Church with two stanzas of a beloved hymn.

> Rise up, O men of God! Have done with lesser things;
> Give heart and soul and mind and strength to serve the King of Kings.
> Rise up, O men of God! The Church for you doth wait,
> Her strength unequal to the task; rise up and make her great.[7]

---

[6] *Matthew* 28:18b-20.

[7] William Pierson Merrill, 1867-1954, Words by permission of the *Presbyterian Outlook*, Richmond, Virginia.

PART II

THE CHURCH'S
MINISTRY
TO THE CRISES
IN LIFE

INTRODUCTION

Anthropologists have traced a remarkable uniformity in various societies throughout the globe. Certain common stresses or crises of life adjustment seem universally to call for social support and moral guidance. Religions have provided "rites of passage" and "rites of intensification" to aid individuals facing such basic issues as birth, puberty, marriage, sin, illness, and death.

It does not surprise us that God has provided, through the Church, ministries to deal with man's needs at these crucial transition points. These are the Sacraments and ceremonies that have always been part of the Judeo-Christian tradition, albeit gradually refined and developed from one era to another.

It was necessary to discuss the Church as the context for these specific ministries of Sacraments and rites in Part I, because these cannot be thought of apart from the Church any more than preaching or worship would be possible apart from the Church. Some find this analysis distasteful because it reminds them of Freud's insistence that all such religious practices were merely a projection of man's needs and the anxieties generated in connection with stress and threat. It makes more sense to turn it around the other way, and say that God, who created man, also provides for crisis needs just as He does for the routine needs of digestion and respiration.

At this point, the psychology of religion can show the rationale or applicability of various sacraments and ceremonies in meeting the needs of individuals amidst the great issues of their lives. It is not the purpose of this discussion to cover all the doctrinal and exegetical questions involved in these sacraments and rites; that is the task of systematic and biblical theology. Pastoral theology is concerned with the meaning and significance of these ministries to the individual as they meet his personal needs, and how these services can best be administered with vital effectiveness. We know that God is omnipotent and His Spirit works where and when He wills; nevertheless, we have a responsibility in the church to use His gifts of grace with informed and consecrated stewardship. At the very least we should not put unnecessary barriers and stumbling blocks in the way of people's receiving such blessings.

The more convinced pastors and lay members become of the great significance of the Church's ministry to the crises of life the more prominent a place these services will have in the church's total program. Instead of somehow fitting them in so they will not interfere with the "regular schedule," other activities will make way for these all-important services. These are the unique services of the Church; they cannot be referred to any other agency in the community. Healing, social welfare, some forms of character training, recreational facilities (yes, even bowling alleys), the Church has been willing to share, refer, delegate, or relinquish entirely to other agencies of a private or governmental nature; but the ministries of Baptism, Confirmation, Holy Communion, Marriage, and Burial, the Church has never thought could be done as well, or at all, by anyone else. Note the life and death struggle between the Communists and the churches of East Germany over the matter of Confirmation. Church leaders know the importance of the Church's being the agency which guides youth into adulthood and sets their standards. If the Church relinquishes its strategic influence at these crucial points, or minimizes its golden opportunities, the rest of life is far more likely to go the path of least resistance into secular patterns and pagan channels of thought and action. Therefore, these ministries must be a major concern of pastoral theology. They are theology in action.

The Church needs to meet man at the various levels of his existence. All would agree that man has bio-physical origins, that psychological developments help to create his unique individuality, that socio-cultural influences shape his personality structure. The church adds that spiritual dimension and religious meaning which gives man's personality value, standards, and eternal destiny. Allport gives the following broad definition of personality:

> Personality is the dynamic organization within the individual of those psychophysical systems that determine his unique adjustments to his environment.[1]

---

[1] Gordon W. Allport, *Personality* (New York: Henry Holt and Company, 1937), p. 48.

The sacraments and rites of the Church do deal with the various levels or elements of man's personality. They are the outward and visible sign of an inward and spiritual grace. They use material elements and deal with man's physical nature on one hand, and with his spiritual and mental nature on the other. They are culturally and sociologically re-enforced in the context of the group (congregation). Above all, they point and guide man through the crises of life to his eternal destiny, back to his Creator.

CHAPTER 7

BAPTISM AND BIRTH

From Roman Catholic educators, who say they would be content if granted the first six or seven years of a child's life, to psychoanalysts, who stress the significance of birth trauma, prenatal influence, and the "oral stage," there is general agreement that one cannot begin too soon in the concern and guidance of personality development. The extreme materialist and behaviorist, John B. Watson wrote:

> Give me a dozen healthy infants, well formed, and my own specified world to bring them up in and I'll guarantee to take any one at random and train him to become any type of specialist I might select—doctor, lawyer, artist, merchant, chief and, yes, even beggar-man and thief, regardless of his talents, penchants, tendencies, abilities, vocations, and race of his ancestors.[1]

There is a note of mechanical determinism here with which Christians would take issue, but the idea of beginning with the "infant" as early as possible is surely reflected in the Church's historic practice of infant Baptism.

In our day, most landlords find that children and dogs depreciate real

---

[1] John B. Watson, *Behaviorism* (New York: W. W. Norton & Co., 1925), p. 82.

estate faster than a nice childless working couple. A child is a modern nuisance in the efficiency apartment of the middle and upper-middle class. With this attitude no wonder so many children are rejected even before they are born. Yet we are confronted by a tremendous increase in the birth rate. How necessary it is that we re-evaluate our attitude toward the child and his advent into the world!

BIBLICAL BACKGROUNDS

The greatest misfortune that could befall the patriarchs of old was to be childless; whereas, to count his blessings usually meant to count his children. God's covenant with Abraham promised him a son and a land. The covenant began with the birth of a son. Much later God went to great lengths to preserve and protect another child, Moses, from a cruel and heartless society, in order that he might grow up to set his people free. By saving a child, God preserved the nation. Samuel was another example of the dedicated child.

In the Old Testament, special religious ceremonies were performed to minister to the child and to the needs of the mother.

> The Lord said to Moses, "Say to the people of Israel, If a woman conceives, and bears a male child, then she shall be unclean seven days; as at the time of her menstruation, she shall be unclean. And on the eighth day the flesh of his foreskin shall be circumcised. . . . And when the days of her purifying are completed, whether for a son or for a daughter, she shall bring to the priest at the door of the tent of meeting a lamb a year old for a burnt offering, and a young pigeon or a turtledove for a sin offering, and he shall offer it before the Lord, and make atonement for her; then she shall be clean from the flow of her blood. This is the law for her who bears a child, either male or female." [2]

We might not approve of the concept "unclean" concerning child birth and menstruation, but there was something honest and straight-forward about this attitude. It recognizes society's inevitable anxiety about a process so mysterious and powerful, the strange mechanism whereby life itself is generated. Contrast our hush-hush attitude and compulsive concern about things sexual with the open attitude of the Old Testament day, yes, even its inclusion in the center of worship, the Temple. Our modern advertisements place great importance on the advantages of sanitary devices that won't let anyone know the secret that "she has difficult days." It was no secret to a Jewish youngster; her mother had gone to the temple to acknowledge before God the mystery of her

---

[2] *Leviticus* 12:1-3 and 6-7.

menstruation and her experience of childbirth by offering a sacrifice just as all the other mature women did.

Circumcision identified the Hebrew boy with the nation; it symbolized his membership in a social solidarity. As a child of Israel, he was a child of God. He had been accepted into this fellowship long before he had had opportunity to earn or merit a place among his people. Since his birth he had been accepted, both religiously and socially. The girls shared this membership through identification with their fathers or as being of "one flesh" with their husbands.

The crucial once-for-all break-through of God into history centered around the Incarnation, the birth of the Christ Child. In Scripture we find much made of this in the Gospels; and in the life of the Church, the Annunciation, the Visitation, the Birth of Jesus, The Circumcision, the Name of Jesus, and the Presentation in the Temple are all celebrated as important events centering around the birth of Jesus. The Christmas story and season is a poignant reminder that Jesus' life here on earth began as ours did through birth: "born of a woman." Jesus' many references to children, blessing them and pointing to them as the ideal type of humility for entrance into the Kingdom of Heaven, indicate that we cannot begin too early in our concern for the young person.

As in Circumcision, so in Baptism, the child is accepted by God and the people of God long before he or she has contributed anything to such acceptance. Infant Baptism is a clear manifestation of the doctrine of Grace. Once it has been clearly grasped in connection with Baptism it is more easily seen in other connections. The infant is accepted by God as being of inestimable worth long before his capacities, skills, IQ, social status, and ultimate personality development are known by society. Just as he has been physically born and accepted into his family, so he must be accepted in the spiritual, psychological, and social sense.

SIGNIFICANCE FOR CHILD AND PARENTS

In the deepest theological sense, Baptism is administered primarily in the interests of the child. "Let the children come to me, and do not hinder them; for to such belongs the kingdom of heaven." [3] Baptism is the entrance into the Kingdom of God and eternal life. In the words of the Great Commission, "Go therefore and make disciples of all nations, baptizing them in the name of the Father and of the Son and of the Holy Spirit. . . ." [4]

Baptism also has great significance for the parents. The parents are deeply involved in the process: they answer on behalf of the child; they

[3] *Matthew* 19:14.
[4] *Matthew* 28:19.

promise to bring the child up in the nurture of the Christian faith, to teach him, to train him in worship, and to integrate him into "communion with the Church." The role of the parents is so important that sponsors or godparents are designated to carry on this function of guidance in case of death or incapacity of the true parents.

The acceptance or rejection of the child on the part of the parents is not some esoteric and mystical phenomenon, nor is it a vague abstraction. It is made up of hundreds of specific acts and quite tangible relationships. Especially in the first days and months, the baby depends upon non-verbal reassurances of a primitive nature. How do parents deal with the bodily functions of nursing and weaning, the changing of diapers and toilet training, the crying and teething, the endless demands and yet the simple "Thank you" not spoken for the first few years? At the very least we could say that parents need all the social support, emotional understanding, and spiritual undergirding that the Church can provide to aid them in the crisis of birth and the stresses of parenthood. Although this is especially true in the birth of the first child, it is also true in varying degrees for all childbirth, for no two births are the same. Even the parents are not the same from one birth to the next; they are older, more experienced, facing different stresses or successes, and more or less capable of handling the crisis of childbirth.

Both educators and workers concerned with mental health tell us how crucial are these formative years and how vital the role of parent is. For the developing infant, the father and mother are the first culture, and the home the first glimpse of the universe. Is it a harsh culture and an insecure universe? If so, it will be hard later in life to pray, "Our Father who art in heaven," with any real trust and love. In the home can be established the earliest outlines of justice, order, and security as the foundation for the upper stories of maturity. Here the basic doctrines of grace, forgiveness, and Christian charity can be acted out and demonstrated long before they are full blown, logical formulations of the intellect.

Baptism is a sacrament, and as such, a means of grace. In a secondary sense, the parents have been given a vital role in mediating and interpreting this grace by the very act of bringing the child for Baptism and living up to the covenant they have made for the child until he has reached the age of discretion and can answer for himself. But they need not do this in fearful isolation. The Church has provided a ministry to assist them in their role of parenthood.

PREPARATION, FOLLOW-UP, AND PASTORAL CARE

We have suggested parents need help, but what kind of help? Without being morbid and alarmist about it, the very fact of recognizing birth as a crisis should help the pastor, among others, to be alert and available at such times. This is a crisis unlike many others because there are many months of preparation and expectation. Wholesome interest on the part of neighbors, relatives, and others is to be welcomed. Unfortunately, genuine concern is often mingled with old wives tales, gory references to monstrosities, birth injuries, "blue babies," and miscarriages.

Granted that not every expectant mother has a "problem," and that wonderful strides have been made in the field of obstetrics, the pastor could be available when discussing arrangements for the Baptism. It should not be taken for granted that expectant couples will automatically think of Baptism until someone else brings it up. Perhaps amidst other matters pertinent to making routine plans and setting the date, the couple will be able to discuss some of their ambivalent feelings concerning the coming event. If there are unresolved negative feelings on the part of the parents, it would be a great help to the child if these could be straightened out before he had to sufer the consequences in his personality development. Unmarried mothers and other "problems cases" get a lot of opportunity to think through the significance of childbirth with the help of social workers and chaplains of girls' receiving homes. Yet many a young married mother has mixed emotions and fears about childbirth which she hesitates to discuss because it "shouldn't have to be a problem." "I ought to be filled with joy and gratitude," as one young mother said.

Many pastors who are very conscientious about calling on the "sick" hesitate to call on new mothers in the hospital routinely. Again, granted that many women have more than enough visitors, and that everything is going along well for them and their babies, it will turn up just frequently enough that the pastor's visit was really needed and thus timely. A few days after the excitement and exhaustion of delivery, the mother might be receptive to a call from the pastor. The following are a few comments that bear further discussion:

> We hadn't planned to have any children till Bill finished Law School. You see I was teaching, and we were counting on that.

> His mother doesn't think I can manage two so young.

> It scares me—having all this responsibility.

> We've prayed and prayed to have a baby, and then she was born dead. What have we done to deserve this?

> We're pretty old and our other children are all in school; then this one came along. But he's cute *anyway.*

> My husband doesn't say much about the baby.

There is a sense in which all the Sacraments and ceremonies of the

Church cannot be fully appreciated or wholeheartedly entered into by the faithful if they are not instructed and prepared. Sermons provide an excellent opportunity to unfold the meaning and vital significance of Baptism, everything from the theological import to the practical details. What are the expectations, policies, requirements, and services of the Church in regard to Baptism? The laity cannot be blamed for not knowing if they have never been instructed.

For example: the mundane and simple question of "perquisites" or gifts given to the minister at the time of Baptism. A perquisite has the connotation of an income over and above one's wages, such as a tip or gratuity. Now really! Does the pastor, who was ordained and called to preach the Word and administer the Sacraments, want to have Baptism interpreted as an "extra-curricular" activity, something above and beyond his "regular ministry," covered by his monthly salary? From the point of view of pastoral theology, the manner in which the pastor structures certain relationships becomes an interpretation of the Church, the pastor's office, and often enough, some doctrine of basic importance. Surely not the slightest opportunity should be offered for mistakenly feeling one is "paying $5.00 for having the baby christened." On the contrary, everything should point to the free gift of grace thereby bestowed. Besides, if someone should feel deep gratitude for this ministry, there is ample opportunity for this to be expressed in gifts toward the Church, which has made provision for this sacrament. In short, the Sacraments belong to the Church, not to the minister. Much embarrassed discussion over a little white envelope offered after the service could be avoided if such policies were publicly interpreted.

Let us be sure that parents and sponsors know what Baptism is all about so that they can speak intelligently and with conviction when they answer in the child's stead and commit themselves to certain promises. Brief tracts, a pastoral call in the home, and so forth will supplement other methods of Christian education in this vital area of the Christian faith.

Baptism must have more careful follow-up than in the past if we are to avoid the large number of lapsed baptized members who never reach Confirmation. Denominations provide Cradle Roll follow-up cards and material to be mailed periodically to parents of small nursery children. There is one caution: no routine plan like this should be undertaken unless it is possible to do it consistently; otherwise there will be some hurt feelings on the part of those who are missed. A Cradle Roll Department Chairman could be assigned this duty, to be reported on periodically. If Baptism is a responsibility of the whole church, it should be the natural concern of lay people as well as a concern of the pastor to follow up on these children.

Many other helps may be made available by denominational Christian education departments, evangelism offices, departments of social missions, and family life educators. The main concern of this discussion is that Baptism not be considered an isolated activity which intrudes itself into the worship service for a few minutes on Sunday morning. If it is as important as the Church maintains, it deserves serious attention, ample preparation, and follow-up in the life of the infant Christian and in the continuing awareness of his parents. We also see that pastoral care is not a separate ministry limited to "counseling cases," but is a resource that precedes, follows, and undergirds all the Sacraments and rites of the Church.

LITURGICAL ELEMENTS AND ARRANGEMENTS

Water was listed by the ancient Greeks as one of the four elements of the universe. The others were earth, air, and fire. Not only is water a basic essential to life, but, as in the case of many basic elements, it has been used to symbolize deep issues of life. "The waters" occurs ten times in the first Chapter of Genesis. While the earth was still without form and void, we read, "the Spirit of God was moving over the face of the waters." Water is a symbol of many things: (a) trouble, "Save me O God! I have come into deep waters and the flood sweeps over me"; (b) joy and praise, "O sing to the Lord a new song. . . . Let the sea roar, and all that fills it, Let the floods clap their hands"; (c) peace and security, "The Lord is my shepherd, I shall not want. . . . He leads me beside the still waters"; (d) purification and righteousness,

> The Lord said to Moses, "You shall also make a laver of bronze, with its base of bronze, for washing. And you shall put it between the tent of meeting and the altar, and you shall put water in it, with which Aaron and his sons shall wash their hands and their feet. When they go into the tent of meeting, or when they come near the altar to minister, to burn an offering by fire to the Lord, they shall wash with water, lest they die." [5]

When written "the water" or used in the plural, the element frequently refers to the amniotic fluid which surrounds the embryo in the mother's womb and cushions it against shock and injury. Psychoanalysts such as Jung feel this first environment gives water much of its symbolic significance. It appears in much folk literature. No wonder this all-pervasive element is used in Baptism to conduct a child into the Kingdom of Heaven, for surely a more all-inclusive symbolic element could not have been found in all God's creation.

How shall we use this water for the "washing of regeneration"? First,

---

[5] *Exodus* 30:17-20.

let us not be ashamed of it and hide it in a corner or try to be too terribly dainty with it. Let the people see the water roll off the child's head and splash into the font again three times as the words are spoken: "_____(Name), I baptize thee: In the Name of the Father, and of the Son, and of the Holy Ghost. Amen." Also speak the question of the naming of the child in a loud clear voice. The whole liturgy of it is a public affair to be done not only in the presence of the congregation in order that they might testify to it, but also that it might be a witness to them and a reminder of their own Baptism. Martin Luther once said that when he was troubled and faint hearted, he took courage in contemplating his Baptism as an historic and objective fact.

This brings to mind the great loss and disadvantage of shunting baptismal services off into a little private affair in a side chapel, and at a time other than that appointed for the main service of worship where it can be witnessed by many of the congregation. In fact, one could wish that in a large church where there are multiple services, baptisms would be scheduled alternately so that everyone would witness this Sacrament. Otherwise, it would be possible for many not to be aware of this sacrament ministry, nor able to lend their social support to, and share the joy of childbirth with, the parents. Official church rubrics urge public Baptism except in extraordinary cases of illness, emergency, or other necessary cause.

> The Minister of every Parish shall often admonish the People, that they defer not the Baptism of their Children, and that it is most convenient that Baptism should be administered upon Sundays and other Holy Days. Nevertheless, if necessity so require, Baptism may be administered upon any other day. And also he shall warn them that except for urgent cause, they seek not to have their Children baptized in their houses.[6]

This latter statement cautions against considering Baptism a private affair; it rightfully belongs in the church and amidst the congregation.

A faithful Altar Guild can help to make certain physical arrangements for the Baptism such as seeing that warm water is supplied in the font, that there are neat and sufficient napkins or small towels for blotting the baby's head after the water has been used, and so forth. Some have provided a small napkin which can be given to the parents as a memento; it may have a cross or other symbol worked into the material. One should avoid too many embellishments or the service becomes cluttered and maudlin, as in the case of one church where the minister used a rose bud to sprinkle water on the baby's head, and then presented the flower to the mother with dramatic flourish and no end of smiling. Avoid adding

---

[6] *The Book of Common Prayer,* The Church Pension Fund, 1936, p. 273.

unnecessary sentimental "gimmicks." But use all legitimate and liturgically correct means to emphasize the dignity, importance, and joy of the occasion.

In large churches there is certainly an advantage in grouping baptisms together once a month or on certain church festivals. Services must not be so closely spaced that baptisms would ever be considered a nuisance or an impossibility in the "regular schedule." If time must be saved, omit an anthem or an optional hymn, but never regular parts of the liturgy of either the Baptism or the Service.

Beyond these admonitions the rubrics in most service books and orders of service are sufficient, and such instructions are there for a justifiable reason in keeping with the theology of the given denomination and its cultural heritage.

RECORDS, RECRUITMENT, AND ROUTINE

Professor Blizzard's study of ministers disclosed that administrative routines were functions in which they felt they were least effective and least interested.[7] This is understandable, and not uncommon among lawyers, doctors, professors, and other professional men, perhaps as much as among clergymen. However, accurate record-keeping and statistics in some areas are more important than elsewhere; Baptism is one of those important areas.

During the compulsory draft in World War II, many clergymen were asked by young men for records of their Baptisms. If other records of their births and ages were unavailable, lost or destroyed by fire, the parish register was accepted as a legal document. Supposedly, there would have been no reason to have entered a false date of birth eighteen or twenty years prior to the time the date was requested by a draft board.

Another instance of the significance of parish records occurred in the writer's experience. A mixed marriage (the wife belonging to the writer's parish A and the husband belonging to another denomination B) produced a son. Some years later the husband killed the mother and was sent to prison for seventeen years. The question arose as to which relatives should be awarded the child in the fight over adoption. The judge felt it was quite crucial evidence that both the father and mother had been present and stood at the font for the Baptism in parish A, and it was so recorded in the parish register several years before. This was accepted as evidence that it was the intention of both mother and father that the faith of denomination A (at the very least the father had not objected at that time) should be the church home of the child.

[7] Samuel Blizzard, "The Minister's Dilemma," *Christian Century*, Vol. LXXII, No. 17, April 25, 1956, pp. 508-10.

Emergency baptisms performed in hospitals by nurses or other lay persons should be recorded not only in the patient's case history at the hospital but also in the parish church of the parents. Such baptisms should be announced in the church for the congregation to hear and witness.

There may be many other instances in which this record is of practical, personal, or legal interest and significance.

Baptism records are of essential importance for recruiting pupils for Sunday School, Week Day Church School, Vacation Church School, youth groups, Confirmation classes, etc. It is a basic starting point for evangelism. The church must be concerned if those whom it has baptized into the faith are beginning to stray away from it. Reference to that person's Baptism would be a natural starting point in discussion of his relationship to the Church. Verily, he is in the Church and his parents intended earnestly (if it was interpreted rightly at that time) that he should remain faithful to the covenant they pledged.

If the Church does not know the names (and addresses) of its members, how can it be an extension of the Good Shepherd who knew His own and called each of His sheep by name?

Baptismal certificates should always be signed by the sponsors and by the pastor. These and any other brochures, booklets, tracts, or mementoes are bought and paid for by the church. If large numbers of children are to be baptized, these certificates can be made out in advance so that only signatures need to be affixed after the service. All this information should be automatically available to the Cradle Roll or Home Department as well as to the evangelism committee of the church. A number of prospect contacts may be made through the ministry of Baptism. There may be relatives and friends of the family who do not come into contact with the Church other than at such occasions. If the Church has ministered meaningfully and effectively to this one family and their child, maybe these spiritually footloose folks will see that the Church has a relevant message and a relevant ministry to the great issues of life. Therefore the guest register should be especially checked on Baptism Sundays to ascertain whether or not these people have a church home.

ADULT BAPTISM

One winces to see congregations regard adult Baptism as an embarrassing reception of new members. Let it be at the font, at least as important as the Baptism as a child. Rather than to minimize Baptism, let us highlight it as a great and dramatic initiation into the Kingdom of Heaven and into the visible Church here on earth. One lady said, "I don't know if he'd want to be baptized right up in front of everyone, it would almost be like suggesting he wasn't a Christian before."

A great danger for the Church in this era of religiosity is that people are likely to "join" the church like they join the 4-H Club, the Masonic Lodge, the Chamber of Commerce, Blue Cross, or a bridge club. As one woman speaking to another member of a church about her membership said, "Well, dear, you know how it is. My Alice finally went off to college, and I had a lot of time on my hands. I felt I did want to get into something more." It would have been a very salutary thing for this woman to have been confronted with the full implications of the doctrine of Baptism. The same "orientation sessions" would hardly be equally suitable for a person transferring from one sister congregation to another within the same denomination, a person going from one evangelical denomination to another, and a person coming into the Church from the world. Would we be too timid to label the latter a "convert"? Greater attention to proper preparation for membership in the Church would go far toward eliminating the drastic losses due to lapsing.

At the very beginning of one's life as a Christian stands the doorway of Baptism. Anything the Church can do to strengthen and intensify this ministry to the crisis of birth and the gracious work of rebirth and regeneration would be effort well spent and strategically placed.

There seem to be no more fitting words with which to close this section on the Sacrament of Baptism than the closing words of the admonition to those who bring a child for Baptism:

> . . . that, abiding in the covenant of his Baptism and in communion with the Church, he may be brought up to lead a godly life until the day of Jesus Christ, I therefore call upon you to answer in his stead.

And then the question:

> Do you present this child to be baptized into this Christian Faith? [8]

---

[8] *Service Book and Hymnal*, pp. 243-44.

CHAPTER 8

CONFIRMATION AND
COMING OF AGE
IN THE KINGDOM [1]

One must leave home as did the Biblical Abraham, leave comfort and security as did the Biblical Moses, i.e., to leave home and go out into the unknown. Man must leave his old supports behind and encounter feelings of temporary isolation, powerlessness, and anxiety. In a real sense this leaving home, this cutting in a more final way the umbilical cord is rebirth, a dying of the old self and a being reborn to new dependencies and limitations. This is a necessity in the process of individuation. . . . But this process does not take place without conflict, tension, and anxiety, because of the misunderstanding of parents, the non-accepting of peers, and the lack of knowledge and contact with the self.[2]

THE MEANING OF ADOLESCENCE

The current emphasis upon adolescence, the "teen ager," and juvenile delinquency makes it necessary for the Church also to focus attention upon this transitional stage of life. The term "adolescence" cryptically sums up the process and problems of this transition. The dictionary traces the implications as follows: *adolescens* is the present participle form in Latin meaning "to grow up" or toward, whereas *adultus* is the past participle, literally having grown up or "having arrived." [3] Does this not characterize the nature of the adolescent's progressive and dynamic development and at the same time describe the condescend-

---

[1] This chapter heading is obviously a paraphrase of Margaret Mead's *Coming of Age in Samoa*. Anthropologists have investigated intensively the religious "rites of passage" and social customs that surround puberty.

[2] Patricia Spencer Stanford, *A Study of the Experiences of Non-Freedom of the Preadolescent*, a Master of Arts dissertation submitted to the faculty of the Divinity School of the University of Chicago, 1954, p. 34.

[3] *Webster's Collegiate Dictionary*, p. 15.

ing attitude of adults who "have arrived" at the much longed for state of maturity? There is also just a hint of fallacy contained therein, because it is not true that the adult has arrived at some static plateau of ideal existence, but is also continually changing and *becoming*.[4] The person no sooner clears the hurdle of adolescence than he must make new adjustments to changed conditions; there loom up upon the horizon the "change of life" in menopause, and later, the slowing down of senility. Yet it must strike us as significant that the transition from childhood to adulthood through the period of puberty is so great a crisis that special attention has been paid to it in the Church through the rite of Confirmation. Some traditions such as the Roman Catholic and Orthodox churches consider it a Sacrament that only a bishop can administer.

In the Old Testament, and in later Jewish tradition, there was a definite ceremonial recognition of the transition in adolescence, a turning point in the life of the boy. Lewis Sherrill describes it.

> A Jewish boy, upon completing his thirteenth year, had reached the age of responsibility and duty in religion, and this stage in his life was attended by ritual acts. At thirteen he was regarded as ripe for the commandments, that is, responsible for his own observance of the Law. He could now make his own vows, and was held accountable for his own sins. In the course of time there came to be a special ceremony called *Bar Mizwah*, or Son of the Commandment, to celebrate the boy's attainment of the age of responsibility in his religion. . . . On the Sabbath of his Bar Mizwah the boy would go to the synagogue, be called to the bema or platform to recite the benedictions, read from the prophets, and perhaps deliver an address. Thus it was, and still is signified that the boy had become a responsible member of the congregation. The ceremony did not make him a member, for he was that already. It was the token of his public assumption of his part as a "man." [5]

Thus, in some ways, similar to the relationship between Circumcision and Baptism, there is in the Old Testament a provision for somewhat the same function to be exercised in the *Bar Mizwah* as we see later expressed in the Christian Church's Confirmation ceremony.

It is of further interest that the one incident mentioned in the life of Jesus between the birth stories and his three-year public ministry is drawn from his adolescence, when he was twelve years old.[6] It is the text for the First Sunday after the Epiphany and could serve as a natural text from which to preach to this condition of life. This is one of the Church's important ministries to a strategic crisis of life.

[4] *See* Gordon W. Allport's *Becoming* (New Haven, Conn.: Yale University Press, 1955).

[5] Lewis J. Sherrill, *The Rise of Christian Education* (New York: The Macmillan Company, 1950), pp. 25-26.

[6] *Luke* 2:41-52.

CRUCIAL GROWTH AND DRASTIC CHANGES

Where there is life there is change. The changes of physical growth are often accompanied by tension, discomfort, and even pain. Consider the stresses of teething and the pain of an infant's gums as the growing teeth push their way through the flesh. During certain periods of anatomical development, the muscles, bones, joints, nervous, and endocrine systems are not in harmonious balance as one part grows and matures faster than another. Such change is characteristic of adolescence. The colloquialism "growing pains" can be quite literally true.

Without taking into consideration the physical base and equipment of the adolescent, we cannot hope to understand his pyschic and spiritual life. The physical clumsiness caused by his drastically changing skeletal and neuromuscular growth cannot help but have its repercussions in social and emotional insecurity. Because he rejects his skin marked by acne (usually temporarily), he assumes that others reject him as a person. Bodily sensations focus attention upon himself and make him self-conscious and sensitive to criticism in a group. These new-found drives and powers are certainly not all negative; they provide the adolescent with vigor, vitality, and enthusiasm, which, if properly harnessed, can accomplish constructive service goals. Many a church has received help and stimulus from a youth group far out of proportion to their numbers.

Perhaps one of the most troublesome and crucial areas of growth is the upsurge of sexual awakening. Here is power to procreate new life and it is an awesome power. Adults shudder to think that this power is given to thirteen and fourteen-year-old "children," and that's the rude awakener —they're hardly children any more if they are capable of becoming parents, as many are. Naturally, such an exciting new power and compelling interest incites adolescents to sexual exploration and experimentation. Masturbation is an almost universal experience of boys and girls during puberty. It varies in intensity, meaning, and frequency. For some it is fortunately only a passing phase, and other more social and less egocentric interests occupy their time and attention. Sports, parties, extracurricular school activities, and interest in the opposite sex bring more rewards than masturbation. However, there are some lonely youths who do not derive rewards and satisfactions from social relations; they have met with so many emotional frustrations, social failures and rebuffs that they return to their one dependable satisfaction, the solace of masturbation, much as an alcoholic returns to his ever-ready bottle. The orientation toward sex in this crucial time may fix patterns that will influence his marriage and social relations for good or ill in later years. It is indeed a crucial time of growth.

Interpersonal relationships may be roughly divided into three stages:

dependence, independence, and interdependence. These should characterize the healthy relationships of infancy, adolescence, and adult maturity.

Dependence is the natural stage of the young of all higher forms of life. Only the length of time varies. Some baby birds can fly and shift for themselves in an amazingly short time, while the baby calf must be suckled by the cow for months. The human infant is totally dependent for a remarkably long time, with no fur to protect him from the elements, and quite unable to walk with any degree of skill and speed for at least a couple years; and one can only speculate how long he could survive in nature without constant dependence upon his parents. This is the stage of life in which security is established as a foundation of personality structure (what Erik Erikson refers to as "trust vs. basic mistrust").[7] One hardly dares experiment with the rebellion of adolescence without this basic security—knowing there is someone upon whom you can depend, someone who loves you enough to protect and care for you. The close correlation between such trust and dependence and one's religious faith need hardly be belabored here. One who has been rocked in the loving arms of parents upon whom he has safely depended can understand such references in Scripture as "the Everlasting Arms."

Independence is the violent but necessary characteristic of adolescence. This is the time when the young boy sharpens his personality against the grindstone of his own father's authority. This causes tension and friction. The only way a colony becomes a nation is through revolution and a declaration of independence. One does not really become a true person without proving himself; without this individuation one is still a sort of appendage, a mere extension of the parents' personalities.

Complex and ambivalent attitudes toward parents, especially the father in a patriarchal society, accompany the struggle of the adolescent for independence. There is a necessary devaluation of the parents. It is not true that "Daddy can do anything." By this age the child has had enough disappointments and has seen his father and mother make enough mistakes, so that he no longer holds the childish and idolatrous notion of parental omnipotence. This need not be a violation of the Fourth Commandment. Parents are to be honored, not worshipped. In infancy and early childhood, the parents have been physically larger and comparatively much stronger, but now the differences are not so marked. By the time of adolescence (let us say 14 years of age), the son may well excel his father in certain physical feats such as swimming, ball playing, and running. The father may even hesitate to threaten physical punishment

---

[7] Erik Homburger Erikson, "Growth and Crises of the Healthy Personality," in *Personality in Nature, Society, and Culture* (second edition), edited by Clyde Kluckhohn and Henry A. Murray (New York: Alfred A. Knopf, 1953), pp. 190-97.

as discipline because of the danger of not being able to follow through against his son who has just won a boxing tournament at the local school. They are becoming a closer match, and the possibility of revolt looms on the horizon. Parents become as anxious as the adolescents about what will come of the rebellion.

How will the child pass through the troubled waters of adolescent revolt in search of independence and individuation? This depends to a large degree upon the parent-child relationships that have been built up over the preceding years. If the parents have been overly possessive and have satisfied too many neurotic needs by having their children helplessly dependent upon them, the price will appear too high, and the parents will resist any danger of "losing their children." On the other hand, secure and emotionally mature parents will not feel overwhelmingly threatened by the increasing demands for independence. In fact, the mature parent can actually look upon such growth quite positively, "I'm glad to see you're growing up and assuming a little responsibility." Parents need a wholesome sense of humor and willingness to admit their own fallibility at this stage. Nevertheless, the pastor and the church's youth program will have to bear in mind that every adolescent under their care is coming through this stormy period in his or her own unique way and with varying degrees of success.

Interdependence is the ultimate goal of maturity because the high value an adolescent places upon independence should be transitory; independence is not enough. Although independence is a necessary stage of development to be passed through, there is a sense in which it is an egocentric standard of values characterized by, "I want my own way." During adolescence the young person is so concerned about his own needs and the strivings toward independent individuality that he is usually not aware enough of other person's needs. It is an era of relative disregard for the feelings and problems of parents and others.

Rugged individualism may have been espoused in America in the frontier days out of necessity, but it is surely closer to the law of the jungle than it is to the mature Christian ethic. After the crude experiments of adolescence, the young adult must learn to give *and* take, to share, to co-operate, to appreciate as well as criticize, and to temper one's own desires with the concern for others typified by the Good Samaritan and the Good Shepherd who would risk all to help the one lost sheep. He must be as willing to let others depend upon him as he is to depend upon others.

In order to understand adolescence in proper perspective, we must know from whence he came (the stage of dependence) and where he is going (the capacity for interdependence) as well as in what phase he now finds himself (independence). Naturally, these three stages of development are not iron-clad nor mutually exclusive, but in the normal personality they should characterize the periods of infancy-childhood, adolescence, and adulthood.

We have considered the physical and social aspects of adolescence. The *economic* responsibilities that begin to loom up upon the horizon for the adolescent also contribute to his uneasiness and the necessity for rapid growth and maturation. Vocational interests become tangible as friends and relatives stop playing guessing games about "What are you going to be when you get big, Billy?" and vocational guidance counselors in high school remind the young pupil that "If you're going to college and medical school, you'll have to take Chemistry 207," or, "If you're planning on being a court stenographer, you'll need Advanced Shorthand and Typing." Perhaps the counselor challenges the student with an interpretation of his vocational aptitude tests by saying, "Your interests and abilities seem to be similar to those people successful in the mechanical trades. Had you ever thought of taking a course in Machine Shop?" Vocational choice means many things to youth, but, among them, is the seriously practical question of one's worth to society—"Is there a productive niche for me in society?" "Will I be able to stand the competition of the adult world?"

Can it really be said that a person is a full-fledged adult until he has begun to make a man-sized contribution in his chosen full-time vocation? This is in no sense a derogatory definition if applied to some well-adjusted medical school student whose father is capable and kind enough to support him during his extensive period of professional training, or a seminarian working his way through school and not ordained into the ministry till he is twenty-four years of age. Yet, in terms of our definition of the adult (see p. 110), we must admit that he has something in common with the adolescent school boy as regards his economic contribution to society and his vocational status.

What might be called "prolonged adolescence" is becoming more and more characteristic of a large percentage of our young people. This period will be lengthened by the increasing demand for specialized and intensive preparation for adult vocations (the trades as well as the professions). There is a growing tendency to keep a higher percentage of youth in school, to get them through college, or at least through a period of community junior college training. Even in instances where applicants are not suited to further academic training, there are social and economic factors at work to keep them out of the labor force in the trend to "educate all for democratic living." There is also the American notion that "all men are created equal" with an unfortunate confusion between rights and capacities. The fact of the matter is that all men are not created with a 120 IQ. Perhaps society ought not to prolong the adolescence of some who are in fact adult at 17.

We must turn our attention to what this discussion of growth, transition, and turmoil means for the Church's ministry to the crisis period of adolescence through Confirmation.

G. Stanley Hall, a pioneer student of the religious implications of adolescence, made a good case for Confirmation or its equivalent in the following words:

> At the age we have indicated (twelve to sixteen), when the young man instinctively takes the control of himself into his own hands, previous ethico-religious training should be brought to a focus and given a personal application, which, to be most effective, should probably in most cases be according to the creed of the parent. It is a serious and solemn epoch, and ought to be fittingly signalized. Morality now needs religion, which cannot have affected life much before. Now duties should be recognized as divine commands, for the strongest motives, natural and supernatural, are needed for the regulation of the new impulses, passions, desires, half-insights, ambitions, etc., which come to the American temperament so suddenly before the methods of self-regulation can become established and operative. Now a deep personal sense of purity and impurity are first possible, and indeed inevitable, and this natural moral tension is a great opportunity to the religious teacher.[8]

When the writer was serving as a parish pastor of a church having many Danish immigrants, he recalls the older members speaking with considerable respect of the dramatic change of status that confirmation signalized in their native Denmark. At that time the young man was entitled to wear men's long trousers in place of his boyish short pants; he was called the equivalent of "Mister" instead of "Master"; and he began his formal apprenticeship in a trade usually away from his parental home. The girls also "went out" to learn the domestic arts in some large home. The upper-class youth left home for the "Academy" and sometimes studied in foreign countries. In this way their socio-economic, as well as physical roles changed simultaneously. Confirmation came a bit later in Europe than in present-day America—sometimes as late as sixteen or seventeen. Society made a "place" for the adolescent and gave him status. Compare this with the amorphous standing of our juvenile youth.

Anthropologists and psychiatrists have shown the necessity for social support and role guidance in the adolescent years. Much of their research has direct bearing upon how the Church can minister through the rite of Confirmation. Bruno Bettelheim's observation of emotionally disturbed

---

[8] Quoted in *Readings in the Psychology of Religion*, edited by Orlo Strunk, Jr. (New York: Abingdon Press, 1959), pp. 160-61.

adolescents and children led him to make comparisons with the findings of anthropologists concerning puberty rites among primitive peoples, as well as some contemporary developments in our own society.

> Certain movements—for example, the zoot suit movement in the United States and other very different youth movements widespread earlier on the continent of Europe—represent youth's spontaneous efforts to deal with inner needs characteristic of puberty for which society does not provide satisfactions. . . . But, further, any age group needs special learning experiences in line with its developmental tasks. Learning about sex relations, mastering them and the emotions and responsibilities they entail, is the learning most germane to puberty. If it is not provided by society, adolescents will seek it among themselves.[9]

Without the carefully structured guidance of a "rite of passage" through adolescence, juveniles will "act out" and experiment on their own, frequently in delinquent and psychically unhealthy ways. It is urgent that the Church minister to the fullest of its potential capacity to this critical stage of life. Confirmation has historically been this ministry.

We see the adolescent's attempts (sometimes humorous, sometimes pathetic) to find security from his peer group through extravagant fads of conformity, be they "bobby sox," "going steady pins," or "rock 'n roll music." Confirmation is most effective when carried out in the context of peer group support. We will have more to say of this later.

We have considered adolescence from physical, social, and economic aspects; but what is the spiritual opportunity of the adolescent as he approaches Confirmation?

CONVERSION AND CONFIRMATION

Conversion is a mountain top spiritual experience for some, especially those who belong to churches where this pattern is expected in late adolescence and required for full communing membership. Other youth, who belong to churches practicing Confirmation and expecting gradual spiritual awakening through a long pattern of Christian education since Baptism rather than a "conversion" crisis, are puzzled when asked by the former group "When were you saved?" or, "Have you had a spiritual experience?" One psychologist of religion classified religious awakening into three types:

> (a) definite crisis (in emotions and attitudes), (b) emotional stimulus (less intense, no special change, but some event recalled as stimulus to

---

[9] Bruno Bettelheim, *Symbolic Wounds* (Glencoe, Illinois: The Free Press of Glencoe, 1954), pp. 105-06.

awaken religious consciousness), and (c) gradual awakening (religious life flows on like a stream, enlarging and growing, striking no obstructions and forming no cataracts).[10]

Is it possible to minister to people in the same church who are having different kinds of religious experiences in adolescence, or must we separate them into various denominational groupings according to their temperaments and experiences? If there appears to be a tendency for conversion experiences to group around this age of adolescence (12-16), if the psychological make-up of the youth seems to lend itself temperamentally toward increased spiritual sensitivity, and if added guilt feelings arising from sexual maturation and conflict with authority make this an especially vulnerable time, it would seem that the Church should exert every effort to utilize the opportunity to minister to this era of crisis?

The "normal curve" in Figure 15 shows the few who are at the extreme ends of the scale and the many who cluster around average. In intelligence and various physical characteristics, the distribution usually follows a "bell-shaped" curve if the sample is large enough. In the other classifications discussed in the following paragraphs, such as the economic, the same pattern will not be exactly reproduced. But, nevertheless, the normal curve is illustrative since in all six categories, it is generally true that there are few at the extreme ends of the scale, and the majority distributing themselves more or less around the middle of the scale. The general significance of individual differences is the main point of this discussion. When one becomes aware of how many variables make up the human personality, the importance of this issue becomes apparent.

The Psychology of Individual Differences is an essential perspective in catechetics, the classes leading up to Confirmation. *Intellectual Capacity* is most obvious in connection with reading ability and grasp of ideas.

Physical development can vary tremendously between teen-agers of the same chronological age. Girls generally develop earlier, especially in sexual maturity.

Emotional expression may be characterized by extremes of extroversion (interest turned outward) and introversion (interest directed inward) also depression-elation, etc.

Social adjustment ranges from dominance to passivity, from the socialite to the "wall flower," an important adjustment in the age when peers are so significant.

Economic status influences choice of friends (perhaps selection of parish), and can be the source of security, rejection, or inferiority feelings.

---

[10] Paul E. Johnson cites E. T. Clark in his *Psychology of Religion* (revised edition), (New York: Abingdon Press, 1959), p. 127.

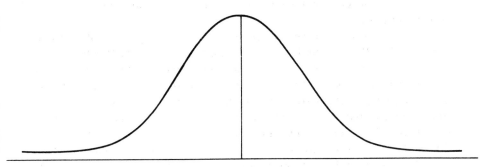

Figure 15. A Normal Curve.

Intelligence:
    Idiot .... Average .... Genius

Physical Characteristics:
    Weak .... Average .... Strong
    Short   Tall

Emotions and Temperament:
    Introvert .... Average .... Extrovert

Social Adjustment:
    Isolation .... Average .... Gregariousness

Economic Status:
    Poverty .... Average .... Wealth

Spiritual Experience:
    Naturalistic .... Average .... Mystical or Other-
                                                                   worldly

Spiritual experience may range from the mystical and ecstatic to the routine, rather unspontaneous, and casual attitude. The form and even capacity for spiritual experience is not unrelated to the preceding five categories.

In perhaps no other age group is it more important to bear in mind the wide diversity of personal capacities and needs than in the adolescent group receiving instruction for Confirmation. In the same class may be young people representative of each of the three types of religious awakening cited above (p. 117f.). Since it is usually not thought wise to depart from the school grade grouping, many of these special cases will have to have special attention. The youth groups and youth choirs supplement the catechetical class with opportunities for further discussion, social action, a great variety of leadership and participation roles. But these cannot be left to chance; they should be co-ordinated and integrated.

Amidst all this concern to understand the complexity of individual personalities, the spiritual goal of Confirmation and its theological relation to Baptism must remain primary. The goal is that each individual young person should grow in the intellectual, personal, and social understanding of the Gospel in all of its glorious relevance to his own soul's welfare that he can make his own confession of faith on Confirmation Day. The element of *Faith* makes catechetical instruction quite different from a ninth grade public school course in American Literature, or Latin. In the public school room, the pupil need only show good citizenship and be relatively co-operative to be "promoted" to the next grade; the matter of conviction, commitment, and anything resembling the personal involvement of faith is usually not considered essential. Confirmation at the end of two or three years of special instruction should not be considered "automatic" in this sense. It is doubtful if there is any other age when the person will be more "ripe" for the kind of spiritual experience (call it "conversion" or what you will) that will make Confirmation a vital ministry in a crucial transition.

PREPARATION, FOLLOW-UP, AND PASTORAL CARE

It is beyond the scope of this work to describe at length the various aspects of catechetics and Christian education that prepare a youth for Confirmation, but it has been deemed essential to show that Confirmation is not an isolated event or *mere* perfunctory ceremony. The amount of preparation for an event usually indicates something about its importance in the minds and lives of those involved. In each of the ministries of the Church to the crises of life, preparation is an essential ingredient.

Professor Granger Westberg has described his ministry to adolescents in relation to Confirmation.[11] He arranged appointments (relatively brief, about 15 minutes each) with all young people who were to enroll in his catechetical class the following autumn. He felt it was important to establish personal pastoral relationships with these pre-adolescents before Confirmation instruction began so that the pastor could be perceived not only as an authoritarian figure, but also as an accepting individual. Pastoral calls in the homes of catechumens could serve the same purpose if the pupil would really believe that the pastor is primarily interested in *him* and not only the "grown ups."

If the specific or immediate seedbed for the Word of God is the

---

[11] An address at the Students' and Pastors' Convocation at Northwestern Lutheran Theological Seminary, January, 1958, Minneapolis, Minnesota.

catechumen, in this case, the home and parental attitudes surely are the garden or the larger context. Parental apathy, lack of enthusiasm and support of the Church's aims, can become the weeds and tares that threaten to choke out the good grain; the harvest will be correspondingly meager. The way in which the public schools have utilized parental interest in education (e.g., the P.T.A.) is a good example for the churches to follow. Many pastors have found it helpful to invite parents (or even require their attendance as a part of the registration procedure) to an orientation session so that the aims and purposes as well as the procedures and lesson plan, homework, etc., can all be explained to the parents and youngsters at the same time. This avoids misunderstanding and keeps the channels of communication open. Most parents are so glad to see someone take this much interest in their children that they will agree to high standards.

Where carefully designed and integrated Sunday School curricula are used, there should be considerable preparation before catechetical classes begin. A foundation of Scripture is being laid; the Gospels have revealed the life and mission of Jesus Christ; and glimpses of the historical development of the Church and its various missions have set the stage for a more comprehensive study by this time.

After the general preparation in catechetical classes has been completed, there needs to be more specific preparation for the actual ceremony of Confirmation. Although the older pattern of public examination was not always pedagogically sound, it at least helped to highlight the event as an important step. Can we substitute something less traumatic and mechanical, but still retain the intensity of interest and attitude of climax that should attend Confirmation? Dramas, posters, a special dinner for confirmands and their parents, a special meeting with the church council to introduce the youth about to be initiated into full communing membership with the official leaders of the congregation, a special reception, opportunities for greetings (perhaps a receiving line after the service of Confirmation together with the pastor at the front door of the church), these and many other methods might occur to the church eager to make Confirmation a memorable and constructive event in the minds of impressionable youngsters.

With the Service Book of the Church in their hands, the young people should have the ceremony and its theological implications carefully explained. Everything should be done to make this a vital, personal testimony of faith. The "Prayer of Blessing" can be solemn as well as joyfully strengthening:

> The Father in Heaven, for Jesus' sake, renew and increase in thee the gift of the Holy Ghost, to thy strengthening in faith, to thy growth in

grace, to thy patience in suffering, and to the blessed hope of everlasting life.[12]

Yet how shall such a grand climax avoid the connotations of a graduation exercise? Too often it is not a commencement of adult membership in the church but a graduation out of the Sunday School. Every effort must be put forth to make a place for these young people in youth groups and choirs, as ushers, in service projects, in challenging and vital Sunday School classes, and in leadership opportunities through teachers' training classes. If the Evangelism Committee has some of these young people on its roster, there will be a natural opportunity to remind them of Communion, worship services, and the commitments they have made in their Confirmation vows: "to abide in this Faith and in the covenant of your Baptism, and as a member of the Church to be diligent in the use of the Means of Grace and in prayer." [13] Youth can best be reached through youth, but it takes the understanding interest of adults to foster an accepting atmosphere in the congregation.

Just as the list of those baptized became a Cradle Roll for follow-up in Sunday School work, so the Confirmation roster becomes a responsibility list. They are now entered in a second membership list in the church book, the list of Confirmed Members, and any of them who fail to appear on the list of Communing Members because they have not received the Sacrament at least once a year, should be followed up soon. But this must be more than a statistical attempt to "keep our membership figures from slipping" or, "showing up poorly in the denominational year book."

An attitude of pastoral care and concern for adolescents should be shown by the church as well as by the minister. How is he doing in school; what are the alternatives in his vocational choice; what line of training is he following for his chosen trade, business, or profession; how does he like college; what has she heard from her boy friend in the military service? These questions and concerns show that the church is as interested in his or her whole life now as during the early years of Sunday School and catechetical classes.

Opportunities for pastoral counseling should be rich and fruitful with this age group, for surely they are tossed about on stormy seas of passion, confusion, intellectual ferment, doubts, idealism clashing with reality, choices, choices, and more choices. Where will they take their problems and where where will they look for guidance? If the church has been helpful in ministering to them through the tumultuous adolescent years,

[12] *Service Book and Hymnal* (Minneapolis: Augsburg Publishing House, 1958), p. 246.
[13] *Ibid.*

there is a good possibility they will continue to come back again and again for forgiveness, guidance, strength, and inspiration. So much will depend upon how they have been initiated into adult maturity, how they have come of age in the Kingdom.

CHAPTER 9

MARRIAGE
AND CREATION
AMIDST FAMILY LIFE

Unlike other animals, man gives birth to fresh offspring while those already born are still entirely dependent on the parents. It follows that a temporary union, having in view the bearing of a single child and terminable when the child is able to go alone, will not suffice; child-bearing goes on for several years, while the firstborn and others are slowly growing to maturity. . . . There results a community of interests, an interlacing of habits. As a consequence of this profound intimacy there appears the singular phenomenon of human love, which touches on the one hand the ordinary sexual desire of the animal world, but extends on the other hand into an habitual affection from which the element of desire may be entirely eliminated. . . . In a word, the human species is naturally constituted in families.[1]

Some form or other of marriage and family life appears to be universal even though its patterns and sanctions may vary from one culture to another. Occupational roles, inheritance provisions, the source of authority and discipline, duties and rights may vary from a matriarchal to a patriarchal system and again may differ markedly from primitive societies to urban American communities; but wherever the researcher goes, he finds some provision for marriage and family life, or at least their equivalents by other names. Anthropologists have studied societies, which at first glance seemed to have no form of marriage and familial structure; but which, on further

---

[1] T. A. Lacey, *Marriage in Church and State* (1912), Revised by R. C. Mortimer (1947) (London: S. P. C. K., 1947), pages 2 and 3.

analysis, proved to have both in such forms as were not easily recognizable to the researcher's frame of reference.[2]

An interesting experiment is being tried in Israel.[3] The agricultural collective called a *kibbutz* is organized for "communal living," where children are raised in community nurseries, and where couples are not "married" in the conventional sense, but merely apply for a larger room which they can share. Even later, when a state-approved "marriage" is formalized (to provide some legal rights for the children), the children do not live with the parents. Since the couple in this communistic arrangement do not own private property, the economic factor usually considered essential to a family is missing. This is a drastic departure from the centuries old pattern of closely knit Jewish family life. In this experiment, not enough time has elapsed to examine the effects on mental health of the children, the spouses, and the community in terms of social organization.

The most serious effort to prove that marriage and the family were not necessary for modern society was made by the Russian Communists in the beginning of their Great Experiment. They were convinced that marriage was a carry-over of bourgeois consciousness and that family life was a device of the Church to perpetuate its reactionary superstitions. Everything was done to weaken the traditional conceptions and expectations of family life.

> Russia, after the revolution of 1917 and until 1944, was a permissive society. Sex relations and marriage were private affairs, illegitimacy carried no stigma, and divorce could be had upon application. . . . New laws passed in 1944 placed greater obligations on marriage and restrictions on divorce.[4]

As an experiment in social control, it seems to have yielded solid empirical evidence in support of the universality and the necessity of the family. Red China also had to retreat from its assault on the family since its massive state-operated nurseries and bare workers' dormitories proved to be too enervating for the morale of the people.

---

[2] *See* E. Kathleen Gough, "Is the Family Universal?—The Nayar Case," in *A Modern Introduction to the Family*, edited by Norman W. Bell and Ezra F. Vogel (Glencoe, Illinois: The Free Press of Glencoe, 1960), pp. 76-92.

[3] *See* Melford E. Spiro, "Is the Family Universal?—The Israeli Case," in *A Modern Introduction to the Family*, edited by Norman W. Bell and Ezra F. Vogel (Glencoe, Illinois: The Free Press of Glencoe, 1960), pp. 64-75.

[4] Ruth Shoule Cavan, *The American Family* (New York: Thomas Y. Crowell Company, 1953), p. 372.

THE JUDAIC-CHRISTIAN MARRIAGE MODEL [5]

The *Genesis* account of creation indicates that marriage began with human society. Marriage is to be considered a result of the Fall, or Original Sin, a kind of concession to man's baser nature. Prior to the serpentine temptation in regard to "the tree of the knowledge of good and evil," it is described in very positive terms as follows:

> Then the Lord God said, "It is not good that the man should be alone; I will make him a helper fit for him. . . ." So the Lord God caused a deep sleep to fall upon the man, and while he slept took one of his ribs and closed up its place with flesh; and the rib which the Lord God had taken from the man he made into a woman and brought her to the man. Then the man said,
>> "This at last is bone of my bones
>> and flesh of my flesh;
>> she shall be called Woman,
>> because she was taken out of man."
>
> Therefore a man leaves his father and his mother and cleaves to his wife, and they become one flesh. And the man and his wife were both naked, and were not ashamed.[6]

This relationship is natural and God-pleasing in keeping with His providence for the human race. Marriage is not merely the plodding duty of fulfilling God's requirement to "be fruitful and multiply." Jesus blessed the wine at the wedding feast in Cana, evidently approving of the joyous occasion. The *Song of Solomon* is a veritable rapture of romance. And in Proverbs we read:

> Let your fountain be blessed,
>> and rejoice in the wife of your youth,
>> a lovely hind, a graceful doe.
> Let her affection fill you at all times with delight,
>> be infatuated always with her love.[7]

Attitudes toward marriage have varied from time to time depending upon emphases within and outside the Church, such as monastic asceticism, the Victorian Era, pietism, and secularism. Often the pendulum has swung from one extreme to another.

---

[5] This is the title used by Floyd Martinson in a section of his *Marriage and the American Ideal* (New York: Dodd, Mead & Company, 1960), p. 37ff. He distinguishes this concept of marriage from the romantic and the rationalistic marriage models.

[6] *Genesis* 2:18 and 21-25.

[7] *Proverbs* 5:18-19.

Marriage partners complement each other. The biblical attitude toward marriage partners saw them as definitely complementing each other rather than in any sense being identically equal. In fact, the advice of the *First Epistle of Peter* would not be very popular in modern America with its stress on equality of the sexes: "Likewise you wives, be submissive to your husbands. . . . Likewise you husbands, live considerately with your wives, bestowing honor on the woman as the weaker sex." [8]

It is a natural consequence of modern democracy's stress on equality that we should accept and respect one another *because,* basically, we are all the same. This is a useful principle where justice is concerned or when we speak theologically of all people being created in the image of God, and, therefore, equal in His sight; but when applied to the characteristics of the two sexes, it is anatomical nonsense, physiologically inaccurate, and psychologically seriously misleading. Accepting people on the basis that they are exactly, or very nearly, like oneself is really not acceptance at all; it is proud arrogance using one's own personality, social mores, physique, sex, temperament, educational standard, vocation, etc., as the criteria.[9] Mature acceptance exists when one can establish rapport and creative interpersonal relationships *in spite of* differences and sometimes even because of them. Just so, heterosexual attraction is based as much on complementary differences as on characteristics that are held in common.

Let us be careful about what we mean when we talk about the "equality of the sexes." Just the fact that both sexes have a right to vote, a right to a jury trial, equal rights to an education and to earn a livelihood, an equal chance to play golf, etc., does not mean that they are "equal" in other significant areas of life. For example, the "weaker sex" happens to live longer. David Abrahamsen, in a popular treatment, provides the following paired lists of characteristics:

MASCULINE	FEMININE
activity	passivity
penetration	receptivity
independence and self-sufficiency	dependency
domineeringness	submissiveness

---

[8] *I Peter* 3:1a and 7a.

See also Gibson Winter's *Love and Conflict* (Garden City, New York: Doubleday & Company, Inc., 1958), Chapter 3, "Father in Fact," and especially his "Note on Husband and Wife in the Bible," pp. 65-68.

[9] *See* the discussion of "The Psychology of Individual Differences" above, pp. 118-119. The Strong Vocational Interest Blank and the Minnesota Multiphasic Personality Inventory, to mention only two personality tests, have male and female profile score sheets as well as a category that indicates the degree of masculinity and femininity of the client.

adventurousness	shyness
logic	intuition
hardness	sympathy
aggressiveness	protectiveness
forcefulness and	flirtatiousness [10]
determination	

It is significant that this contemporary psychiatrist characterizes masculinity and femininity in much the same tone as Scripture. It is only an arbitrary frame of reference that would give one column of traits superiority or greater value than the other. It would be as foolish as asking which were more important, a nut or a bolt, in holding two metal beams together. There has been a weird confusion of sex roles in modern society, that while great stress has been placed upon the physical distinctiveness of the sexes (e.g., pornographic literature, the female form in advertising, etc.), the social and psychological distinctiveness of the two sexes has been de-emphasized. This is most clearly seen in occupational roles, in certain extreme clothing styles, attitudes toward motherhood and working mothers (of young children), and social amenities.

The Church could render a real service to marriage and family life by re-enforcing mutual appreciation of the complementary nature of the relationship between the marriage partners. The Church should not hesitate to mold public opinion in this regard.

Marriage is an enduring relationship. While Jesus cited the Old Testament concept about leaving father and mother and the two becoming one flesh, he added another dimension: time. "What therefore God has joined together, let not man put asunder." [11] Jesus also re-emphasized the prohibitions against divorce [12] interpreting Mosaic Law.[13] Marriage is intended for life. This principle greatly supports those who are married with a feeling of security, as well as serving as a safeguard for social stability, protecting society from becoming unduly burdened with dependent children and disorganized and disrupted families.

> The individual marriage may be the concern primarily of the spouses. To ensure the stability of marriage as an institution is the urgent concern of the community.[14]

[10] David Abrahamsen, *The Road to Emotional Maturity* (Englewood Cliffs, New Jersey: Prentice-Hall, Inc., 1958), p. 149.

[11] *Matthew* 10:9.

[12] *See* Jesus' discussion with the Pharisees in *Matthew* 19:3-9.

[13] *Deuteronomy* 24:1-4.

[14] H. R. Hahlo, *Marriage, Divorce and the Legal Status of Married Women, A Study in Comparative Law,* Inaugural Lecture delivered by Professor H. R. Hahlo at the University of Witwatersrand, Johannesburg, on May 7, 1947. (Johannesburg: Witwatersrand University Press, 1947), p. 30.

The author shows the influence of external factors on the stability of marriage. "In

Whether we look to society or the individual spouses to make marriage an enduring institution, there have been various factors relied upon to strengthen the bond. Perhaps the oldest factor is the dowry or purchase concept of marriage. In this case the bride became the husband's property, and property rights were involved.

> It is a well-established result of recent researches that the Greek marriage law—like those of other nations, Indo-Germanic as well as non-Indo-Germanic, whose social system was patriarchal—started with the purchase concept of marriage. This system was replaced, in comparatively early times, by that in which the bride, together with a προῖξ, was given to the husband by the person who had *potestas* over her without any requirement of a consideration or a nuptial gift from the husband . . . the new system, far from being fundamentally at variance with the former, came into existence through evolution due to a change of economic conditions.[15]

Yet this bargain was not struck as between individuals like a simple sale of an animal or piece of cloth. "The classic Greek family law was private as well as public; and its connection with the political and sacral organization of the *polis* was its strongest support." [16]

Although we would consider such "purchase" marriage too close akin to slavery, it did, nevertheless, provide the essential ingredient of stability and durability. Our whimsical approach of falling in and out of love needs something to give marriage some objective support and longevity. This is provided for in Christian marriage by the commitment of the *will* as well as the commitment of love. As powerful as the emotions are in uniting people in human relationships, they are not, in and of themselves, dependable enough. Feelings must be tempered by reason just as love must be counterbalanced by justice. To provide this stabilizing

---

times of peace and stability, family life too, is peaceful and stable. In times of social unrest, moral decline, and oddly enough, material prosperity, the divorce rate goes up. Life in big cities promotes the incidence of divorce. So do wars and their aftermath. . . . [The stability of family life] depends on the general conditions and temper of the time." P. 30.

For another emphasis, we turn to an author who goes below the superficial level of legal reforms and external pressures in search of stability: John H. Mariano, *A Psychoanalytic Lawyer Looks at Marriage and Divorce*, published by the Council on Marriage Relations, Inc., 110 East 42nd St., New York City, 1952. "Not only is the institution of marriage greatly weakened today, but the true reasons for such conditions remain generally obscured. . . . The major causes for marriage weakness and failures rest basically *inside* the individual." [*From his preface.*]

[15] Hans Julius Wolff, *Written and Unwritten Marriages in Hellenistic and Post-classical Roman Law*, published by the American Philological Association, Haverford, Pennsylvania, 1939, Lancaster Press, Inc., Lancaster, Pennsylvania, Philological Monographs, Number IX, pp. 76-77.

[16] *Ibid.*, p. 82.

character, the Roman Catholic Church has looked upon marriage as a sacrament with special objective grace bestowed for the special responsibilities inherent in the vocation of marriage. Others have looked upon marriage as a contract with long-term legal implications. Lacey lists the following criteria:

> These five conditions, then, are required for a valid contract of marriage. The parties must intend true marriage; they must be physically capable; they must be acting freely; under no constraint and under no mistake; they must be subject to no previous bond of marriage; and they must not be too near akin.[17]

These criteria lift marriage out of the simply passionate or emotional category and add the necessary ingredient of a deliberate, carefully thought out act of the will. The *consent* of the two parties does not mean that the other factors, such as love, witnesses, etc., are unimportant, but it does highlight the role of reason and will in marriage. Such a line of thought lays the necessary foundation for premarital education or counseling, which will be discussed later in this chapter.

Marriage is exclusive by nature. Just as it appears in social groups that a certain amount of exclusiveness tends to stress the in-group feeling and a sense of loyalty, so in the family and marriage relationship, there have been erected strict barriers and limitations. The strictest is the commandment, "Thou shalt not commit adultery." As cited above, Jesus allowed the fact that adultery was so destructive to the marriage relationship that it alone could be a basis of divorce. We read in *Hebrews* 13:4, "Let marriage be held in honor among all, and let the marriage bed be undefiled; for God will judge the immoral and adulterous." The tabu on sexual relations outside of marriage as well as before marriage with the strong social support of premarital virginity help to intensify the uniqueness and exclusiveness of the marriage relationship.

With keen intuitive insight, the Hebrew word for sexual intercourse also means "to know" a person. Hence we read in *Genesis*, "Now Adam knew Eve his wife, and she conceived and bore Cain. . . ." Spouses have a unique and exclusive knowledge of each other and their personality characteristics that is not available to others. Since sex is so pervasive and symbolic of other aspects of personality, it is quite understandable how this etymology developed.

Property rights and inheritance rights are also highly dependent upon the marriage and family relationships. Although our modern kinship regulations may not appear to be as arbitrary as in some past societies, many a court case has shown we still attribute much significance to kin-

---

[17] T. A. Lacey, *Marriage in Church and State* (fully revised and supplemented by R. C. Mortimer in 1947), (London: S. P. C. K., first published in 1912), p. 28.

ship rights. Even permission to perform an autopsy in a hospital is sought according to certain priorities of kinship relationships. All this stress on kinship helps to strengthen the marriage bond and support family life, for marriage is in many senses an exclusive relationship.

SANCTION AND FULFILLMENT OF PSYCHOSEXUAL NEEDS

> There is thus given by marriage grace to extinguish the flames of con-cupiscence. Those whom God calls to the exceptional state of virginity receive the special grace of continence; to the rest of mankind is pro-posed the ordinary grace of marriage, directed to the same end, the pro-duction of the supernatural virtue of chaste living. By reason of its sacra-mental efficacy, marriage is not less chaste than virginity.[18]

> To the unmarried and the widows I say that it is well for them to re-main single as I do. But if they cannot exercise self-control, they should marry. For it is better to marry than to be aflame with passion.[19]

The number of jokes and cartoons centering around the bride and groom, the wedding night and honeymoon, as well as the mar-riage ceremony itself stem largely from the fact that marriage is a crisis. For that very reason the Church needs to minister very knowingly and appropriately to persons passing through this considerable transition. Consider the moral about-face and the drastic change in social pressure: prior to marriage—no sexual intercourse because one of the most disgrace-ful tragedies to befall a young girl or woman is to have a child out of wedlock; after the marriage—interested aunts and grandparents-to-be scrutinize the woman's figure and speculate on the happy probabilities that "a little one is on the way." A more complete and sudden reversal of social expectation could hardly be imagined. The Church and its ministry would be naïve to under-rate the emotional adjustment involved and the amount of help needed for the parties involved. Marriage provides the support needed to pass from the stage of tabu to full-fledged heterosexual responsibility. And although there are those who do not become married, it is strongly expected and encouraged and considered the social norm in our society for adults.

The first thing God said to Adam and Eve was, "Be fruitful and multiply, and fill the earth and subdue it. . . ." [20] Long before Freud analyzed the dynamics of sex, and long before Alfred Kinsey and his researchers made their elaborate statistical tabulations, philosophers, poets, mystics,

---

[18] *Ibid.*, pp. 47-48.
[19] *I Corinthians* 7:8-9.
[20] *Genesis* 1:28.

song writers, dramatists, religious leaders, and the man on the street were quite aware that the sexual drive or instinct was a great preoccupation of the individual in society. It is awe-inspiring to the primitive native as well as to the sophisticated medical student. Just as the will to live is apparently basic to the individual, so sex represents the instinct of the preservation of the race. Here is a mysterious partnership with God in creation itself.

Any power so strong and mysterious and pervasive is bound to arouse mixed feelings of anxiety and great satisfaction. Sex ranks with hunger and thirst in its power and demand for satisfaction. According to the very nature of men and women, it was inevitable that some socially constructive and acceptable means of sex expression be devised.

> Marriage offers, in theory at least, the ideal opportunity for the physical expression of love since social conventions and legal protection concur in keeping the anxieties of unconventional relations away from the partners. Those living in a religious marriage furthermore may find in faith security against anxiety which no worldly forms of protection can equal.[21]

We must speak of "psycho-sexual needs" because the sexual relationship involves the whole personality, mind, emotions, conscience, and interpersonal relationships of the individual participants. Therefore, disturbance of the sexual relationship between man and wife usually is associated with disturbed relationships within other spheres of one or both of the partners' lives—loss of ego-support, tensions, anxieties, threat to security, stress, etc. As the psychiatrist, Gotthard Booth, has said,

> A new partner for sex seems to promise relief, often without awareness of the nonsexual origin of the desire. When a businessman falls in love with his secretary, my usual experience has been not that she is more attractive than his wife, but that his business is failing.[22]

As a generalization for pastoral care in marriage relationships, it is usually more fruitful for the pastor to look upon sexual problems as symptoms rather than as causes of marital difficulty. It is even more safe to assume that there is mutual relationship between general marital adjustment and the adequate fulfillment of psycho-sexual needs.

Gibson Winter has coined a helpful phrase, "the covenant of intimacy," [23] which describes the companionship, the mutual trust, the sharing that accompanies true Christian marriage. Here the pressure of the

---

[21] Gotthard Booth, "The Meaning of Sex—Psychosomatic Aspects of Love," in *Sex and Religion Today,* edited by Simon Doniger (New York: Association Press, 1953), pp. 133-34.

[22] *Ibid.,* p. 134.

[23] *Op. cit.,* Chapter 4.

competitive marketplace, the public pretense of constantly "putting the best foot forward," the role playing associated with one's vocation, and the image one feels he must present to the outer world, can all be exchanged for the spontaneous sincerity and humble honesty toward the trusted lover. When marriage cannot provide at least a fair share of this wholesome atmosphere for personal re-creation, then it is not Christian marriage in the proper sense; then marriage, too, becomes another game of pretense, competition, and sham. If God desires "truth in the inward parts," Christian marriage should be the ideal laboratory for working this out. Marriage has the capacity to foster the greatest fulfillment of the partners' whole personalities in physical, emotional, spiritual, and social areas of growth.

THE SOCIAL AND EDUCATIVE SIGNIFICANCE OF THE FAMILY

When a group of three hundred ministers were surveyed as to what kinds of problems were most frequently brought to them, they unhesitatingly put marriage and family problems at the head of the list.[24] Later, when asked to be more specific, the picture became very diverse, because these problems included delinquency, alcoholism, young unmarried parents, hostility against authority, unwanted elderly people, poverty, housing, and illness. That is precisely the strategic significance of family life—that so many destructive problems have their origin and cause in weak marriages and inadequate family life; and then in turn these forces tend to undermine family life still more. It can become a vicious cycle as every social worker knows.

On the other hand, wholesome Christian family life is the setting for the happiest times, the noblest aspirations, and the most thrilling experiences of life here on earth. Family reunions and birthday parties, the family gathered around the Christmas tree, the birth of a new baby, the rapture of sexual intimacy, love, loyalty, co-operation and mutual helpfulness reach their highest expression through the bond of marriage and daily family life.

The family is a miniature model of society, and all the great issues of life are found there, be they political, economic, or social. When Christians marry, they enter into a laboratory to test out their faith as it relates to these major categories. We may relate these issues to various parts of the Apostles' Creed for the sake of a common point of departure.

"I believe in God the Father Almighty . . ." Not only do man and wife

---

[24] "Inventory of Health and Welfare Needs and Services" conducted by the Lutheran Welfare Society of Minnesota in 1955. *See also* "Danger Signals in Family Life," in the Society's publication, *Link*, Vol. 11, No. 3, June, 1957, pp. 3-6.

exercise power in the creative process of begetting children, but the questions of power, authority, control, discipline, in short, the political issues of human relationships arise again and again within the family. Paul wisely writes to Timothy, "Now a bishop must be above reproach. . . . He must manage his own household well, keeping his children submissive and respectful in every way; for if a man does not know how to manage his own household, how can he care for God's church?" [25] The time one is most likely to be thought of as "almighty," or having unlimited power, is when parents are dealing with their little children. Representative of this relationship is not only the proud, "My Daddy can do anything," but also the fearful dread of what this "all-powerful" adult might do if his temper tantrum continues. Children can try the patience of parents as much or more than the worst conflict at an adult bargaining table. The fact that the all-important element of power is so unequal makes the problem of how to deal with power even more difficult.

Under the First Article of the Apostles' Creed, the doctrine of Providence says significant things about God's relationship to the universe. In the family, parents and children experiment with the use of property, the stewardship of money, and sound planning for the future. In our era of economic and material irresponsibility, the Church could serve families well by helping them to deal with property, money, indeed, all of God's creation more in keeping with the Christian view of life. A Roman Catholic parish in the Bronx, New York, found family life so riddled by exploitative and crafty loan sharks that it established a parish credit union to help educate its people in responsible Christian stewardship. Many families were guided back to economic stability through this ministry.

The Second Article of the Creed deals with Reconciliation. Two great parables of Jesus concerning forgiveness and reconciliation are drawn from family life. The first is the parable of the Prodigal Son so well known to all. The second explains that if one remembers before the altar, in the midst of worship, he has ought against his brother, he should go first and be reconciled with him, and then return and offer his gift at the altar. In the intensity of close relationships there is always the danger of disruptive conflict and misunderstanding, sibling rivalry, jealousy concerning parental favoritism (as in the case of Joseph and his brothers) real or imagined, the ambivalence of love and hate in the same bosom. What better place to demonstrate the effectiveness and therapy of forgiveness and grace than in the Christian family. And, if it cannot work in this intimate and primary group, how should one expect it to work elsewhere—at school, at work, between races, or between nations.

The work of the Holy Spirit is Sanctification—growth in grace. Christian couples grow in love. From the heady raptures of the romance of engage-

---

[25] *I Timothy* 3:2a, 4, and 5.

ment, they discover that their love becomes deeper and more meaningful as the years go by. If they have become less selfish in their marriage and family life, they will no doubt have become more mature in other areas of life as well. Material and sensuous perceptions become enriched by spiritual significance and connotation. What was once largely physical attraction has become increasingly tempered by emotional, psychological, and social meaning. What was initially often a self-seeking and ego-centric concern has become increasingly a matter of self-giving and altruism. To quote Lacey again, as we did at the beginning of this chapter (p. 124), ". . . there appears the singular phenomenon of human love, which touches on the one hand the ordinary sexual desire of the animal world, but extends on the other into an habitual affection from which the element of desire may be entirely eliminated. . . ." In family life there is the opportunity to grow from simple *eros*, through *philos*, to at least an enlarging share of *agape*—growth in grace. This is the highest form of education; and the family is the best school for it.

Belief in the Holy Ghost implies also belief in, and relationship to, "The Holy Catholic Church, the Communion of Saints"; for salvation is necessary for society as well as for the individual. Interpersonal relationships must also be sanctified, must be made holy. In the Christian family, as previously mentioned, we have society in miniature. Fritz Kunkel referred to the mother-child relationship as the primary "we-group." Later this expands to include father, brothers, sisters, aunts and uncles, grandparents, and cousins. If the patterns have been wholesomely established within the family, it is very likely that the "we-group" will continue to expand in ever-widening concentric circles of brotherly love and human fellowship. If the initial "we-group" is endangering, unrewarding, and painful, he may never venture into creative fellowship with others, and may remain stifled as a psychopathic or sociopathic invalid. Anything the Church can do to prepare people to make the most of the social and educative functions of the family will be time and energy well invested in the Kingdom of God.

PREMARITAL PREPARATION

Before solemnizing a marriage, the Minister shall counsel with persons about to be married. . . . The Minister may publish the Banns in the Church, one or more Sundays before the day appointed for the Marriage. . . . All arrangements for the Marriage service shall be made in consultation with the Pastor. . . . Due reverence shall be maintained in the preparation for, and the celebration of, the marriage. . . .[26]

[26] Selections from the rubrics preceding the "Order for Marriage," page 270 in *Service Book and Hymnal of the Lutheran Church in America* (Minneapolis: Augsburg Publishing House, 1958).

Many churches have formal statements indicating that ample preparation for the marriage shall be provided. Yet there is likely a great latitude in practice. If our foregoing discussion has helped to highlight the significance and central importance of Christian marriage and family life, then the Church should be eager to seize every opportunity to get the couple started properly in this vital relationship. Yet many ministers still limit the preparation to the barest minimum of "arrangement" details, such as time, place, and the legal requirements of the state.

Others have proposed detailed questionnaires, psychological testing, a large number of interviews, and so forth as though every couple were in need of depth therapy and applying to a one-man mental health clinic with stained glass windows. Not only would few ministers have the degree in clinical psychology that should qualify them for such an ambitious program; but a very small number of "clients" really need it. A functional program of premarital counseling lies somewhere between neglect and going overboard. Each minister must arrive at a helpful program that includes the needs of the couple and lies within his own professional competence.[27]

Bethesda Hospital, Saint Paul, Minnesota, has established a group method of premarital preparation to which pastors of its supporting constituency, the Augustana Lutheran Church, may refer engaged couples. The Roman Catholic Church has had considerable experience and success with its "Pre-Cana Conferences." Such group methods have the advantage of being able to draw upon specialists and consultants such as physicians, social workers, home economists, hospital chaplains, and marriage counselors.

The need for individual pastoral guidance would be influenced by the availability of such programs. If such services are not available, the following program is suggested, with variations to suit individual needs: three interviews dealing with the social, economic, emotional, physical, and spiritual significance of marriage. The sequence need not be rigidly fixed in the mind of the pastor. The writer found it most natural to begin where the couples' interest seemed to be most obvious. As in all counseling or education, we need to begin where the "client" is and proceed from there.

Social background is often a natural and informal place to begin. How did they meet? What social relations and friendship circles do they have in common? It is useful to discuss the reactions that each has toward the other's family, social status, likes and dislikes in recreation. What of their

---

[27] Granger Westberg's booklet, *Premarital Counseling: A Manual for Ministers,* is a brief helpful treatment of the subject. It is published by the Department of Family Life, Division of Christian Education, National Council of the Churches of Christ in the U. S. A.

educational backgrounds? The pastor does not need to pry this information out of most couples, because they volunteer such common interests. If they grow suddenly silent or get into arguments over some of these social matters, it is even more important that these tensions be brought out in the open and resolved before the marriage rather than trusting that "love conquers all."

Economic planning is often overlooked, especially among young couples who feel their great romantic love soars high above such petty materialistic details as rent, grocery bills, short term loan payments, and health insurance (which usually doesn't cover maternity expenses for at least nine months). The best economic barometer for the man is his vocational status. For the woman, household management is important. Has she done any serious and realistic thinking about a budget for household needs? Does she expect to be supported by this young man in the first year of marriage on the same level that her father has finally achieved after thirty years of hard work? Have they discussed checking accounts, savings plans, life insurance, whether to buy or rent a home, how often they'll trade their old car for a new one, and a dozen other topics that can help each one understand the other's expectations and ambitions? Martinson wisely suggests:

> Couples may not think of budget discussions as discussions of values, but they are. It will help clear the air and hold down the tempers if they realize that they are having a realistic discussion on what they want out out of life rather than an argument over money.[28]

Physical aspects of marriage could very naturally proceed out of the previous discussion. It is a natural transition to raise the question of planning for children after having discussed more general planning. "Have you discussed how many children you would like to have in your family?" Planned parenthood and the attitude toward having children at all are topics of vital interest to couples in the latter part of their engagement— or at least should be. It is not safe to assume one's fiancé has the same attitudes as oneself without discussing it. If these issues are being dodged, it is even more urgent that they be brought out and faced. Here is the ideal time to raise questions about a physical examination, preferably a true discussion with the physician (especially for the bride) and not just a routine blood test, which the state law may require. The pastor does not shun questions about sex, but recognizes that the family physician is the expert in certain aspects. Meanwhile, the minister will provide the Church's view of sex and help the couple come to a wholesome psychological attitude and religious interpretation. The minister cannot do

---

[28] *Op. cit.,* p. 470.

this if he himself is uneasy, anxious, or guilt-ridden in this area. In fact, if he is greatly threatened by this aspect of marriage, it is even more necessary that he rely heavily on the physician, but it is to be hoped that he has resolved his own feelings about the sexual aspect of life, lest "the blind lead the blind."

It goes without saying, that the pastor should be sensitive to the needs of the couple and not belabor points that the couple has long ago resolved for themselves. Also, he will notice areas that bear further discussion. If these interviews are a week apart, the couple will have had opportunity to discuss or think about some of these issues, and may wish to pursue some topic a bit further. It would be unfortunate if the pastor's schedule were so rigid he could not adapt himself to their tempo. It would be useful to have brief pamphlets and tracts on these topics to give the couple to read between visits; a great many are available and should be included in the pastor's literature budget (provided by the church) or in the parish lending library.

Emotional differences should be discussed and may already have been touched on in the area of sexual adjustment—the differences in temperament and emotional needs of men and women. Are they aware of each other's extroversion or introversion, mood swings, temperamental outburst, interests, etc.—the characteristics that make up their unique personalities? Perhaps in their courting days they were so eager to please and fearful of losing each other that they always wore a protective mask over their true feelings. This accounts for many a rough and disillusioning first year of marriage, for in the intimacy of a small apartment and constant companionship, they cannot keep up the sham and finally blow up in frustration. They must be encouraged to be honest with each other. The warm, accepting atmosphere of a pastor's study may be a safe place to begin expressing feelings that had hitherto been considered too threatening. Naturally, the pastor's attitude and ability to elicit honesty can make or break this opportunity. It would be better to break off then, in spite of the broken plans and heartache of readjustment, than to become divorced four years from then and bring added suffering to an innocent child or two.

Spiritual and theological interpretation (albeit in layman's language), is surely the pastor's task. This should make the big difference between a church wedding and one before the justice of peace (*see* Chapter 2). The Marriage Service itself would serve as a good outline for discussion. Emily Post's etiquette (as nice as it is to have things done politely and in good order) ought not overshadow the significance of the meaning of the liturgy and the spirit of worship in this great event. Unhurried discussion of the Scriptural passages, vows, and prayers will put the entire ceremony in the proper perspective. And how do they plan to implement the religious significance of their marriage and family life? Do they have a church home? Mixed marriage problems would no doubt already have been touched on under social backgrounds, but could be further clarified here. If one or the other is changing membership, why not have such instruction before the marriage rather than hoping it will be taken care of "some other time." The material from the previous sections of this chapter might very well enter the discussion. Even if the pastor knows the couple because they have been brought up under his own catechetical instruction and in the church's youth groups, what better time for review and Christian education?

The main import of all these sessions is to show the couple in a practical way that the Church thinks marriage is so important a matter that it deserves this much of the pastor's busy schedule. The more the Church cares the more the young couple will care.

Does the pastor marry all comers like Marryin' Sam in the Li'l Abner comic strip? That laughable caricature has cheap weddings for 50 cents and deluxe affairs for up to two dollars. The same advice is given in this regard as was suggested concerning perquisites and fees for Baptisms (*see* p. 104). The Church has a great responsibility when a pastor presumes to pronounce the blessing upon a marriage. The pastor should not hesitate to refuse if he feels he must do so in good conscience. To do otherwise for fear of criticism or loss of a few members from the church rolls is cowardly. The rationalization, "But they'll only go somewhere else anyway," is definitely out. Just as surgeons are restrained from performing unethical operations so ministers must be equally scrupulous. The high divorce rate in America speaks for itself.

REHEARSAL, GROUP SUPPORT, AND FOLLOW-UP

The minister who is unsure of his pastoral authority and professional competence, and who asks, "Where do you want to stand?" or, "Now who wants to do what when?" or, "Aunt Hannah, don't you think Susan came in a little too fast?", will find his wedding rehearsals running up to two hours or more. Everyone's nerves will be frazzled almost beyond repair. What was intended to be a great ceremony of support, a "rite of passage" in the anthropologist's language, a helpful and positive send-off into a new life of adult responsibility, can become the stumbling stone of nervous exhaustion and the obstacle to a successful honeymoon. It is a little late and perhaps unnecessary to "teach" a twenty-one year old bride how to walk. The purpose of the rehearsal is rather to clarify the procedure, to make the participants more secure and comfortable, and to avoid unnecessary confusion. The more calm, self-assured, and direct the pastor is, the more likely it is that such a useful goal will be achieved. The whole ceremony can be briefly outlined, run through twice, and concluded within half an hour. They can arrive at the bridal dinner on time.

Some festive feasting, congratulatory visiting, and general social support from friends as well as family should be provided for through a reception. If there are not relatives available to arrange this, the congregation should see that it is done. This is no time to withhold hospitality from strangers or people with little social backing. Two specific illustrations will show the proper attitude.

The pastor of a church with four thousand members gave the following rationale for their spacious and graciously appointed lounge. It was to serve as the parlor for those who did not have the space in their own homes for great festive occasions such as wedding receptions, anniversaries, and so forth, or who could not afford the facilities of hotel and country club banquet rooms. Various circles of women's groups were available to cater such affairs. No one need be denied the social supports needed at such festive occasions either because of lack of funds or lack of "contacts."

Another example of fellowship may be cited from a small church of just over a hundred members. The fellowship needs were met in the same one-room basement where everything from Sunday School and youth groups to the annual congregational meeting was held. A young woman was to be married to a Navy man on relatively short notice. The three interviews were still arranged for and there was no impediment to the marriage. Yet the many months that many couples have to prepare for a church wedding were not available. The first impulse might have been to make everything very simple, perhaps at the bride's home or at the parsonage with as little "fuss" as possible. The pastor took for granted it would be in the church and acted on that assumption. Meanwhile, a few women prepared cakes, coffee, and a few simple decorations. After the wedding service and reception, the couple were thrilled that the congregation had cared so much. About sixty members of the little church had come out on a Saturday afternoon on relatively short notice to share in this fellowship. Nothing could have done more to heighten their loyalty and love for the church than this type of genuine concern.

Follow-up pastoral calls in the home of the newlyweds will be most welcome and will remove any suspicion on the part of the couple that the pastor's interest in the wedding plans has been merely perfunctory concern over liturgical adiaphora. About a month or so after the couple return from their honeymoon, the minister could stop by for a brief informal visit. With such a solid foundation laid for their marriage by the church, it is quite likely that, if any problems or distress should arise in the future, they will know where to go for help and marriage counseling if they need it.

The minister will need to familiarize himself with the state laws and local regulations, because in this more than in any other area of his ministry he is a servant both of the Church and of the state. His marriage service has civil status and must be registered in the local county seat or at the state capitol. He must usually file his ordination papers with the authorities upon his arrival in the new community before he performs any marriage. There are many other concerns and special questions that pertain to the whole ministry at the time of marriage and later to the family, but they lie beyond the scope of this cursory discussion.

CHAPTER 10

HOLY COMMUNION
AND CONTINUING CURE

So I find it to be a law that when I want to do right, evil lies close at hand. For I delight in the law of God, in my inmost self, but I see in my members another law at work with the law of my mind and making me captive to the law of sin which dwells in my members. Wretched man that I am! Who will deliver me from this body of death? [1]

If we say we have no sin, we deceive ourselves, and the truth is not in us. If we confess our sins, He is faithful and just, and will forgive our sins and cleanse us from all unrighteousness. [2]

Experience tells us that "missing the mark" (ἁμαρτία—one of the New Testament words for sin) is a universal experience. Even the proudest man will admit, when he is taken off guard and his defenses are down, that he has made some mistakes, that he has passed up some golden opportunities to do great and good things, that he doesn't always do what he "ought." This difference between the "ought" and the "is" in a man's life may be called wrong-doing, failure, defeat, a problem, error, an offense, a misdemeanor, a crime, a violation of the social mores, and so forth, but to the theologian it all boils down to the same thing: sin.

Sin, as a continuing condition and as a series of recurring acts, needs a continuing treatment. Only a few small sects teach the ultimate perfectability of man in this life. Two world wars, a rising crime rate, and a casual reading of the daily newspapers have left relatively few naïve persons who believe in the innate goodness of man. The Holy Communion is the Church's continuing cure for the malady of sin.

[1] *Romans* 7:21-24.
[2] *I John* 1:8-9.

If we have been justified in referring to confirmation and marriage in the anthropologists' term, "rites of passage" from one stage of life to the next, Holy Communion could be described as a "rite of intensification." It is spiritual support to a person in the midst of a crisis which can come at any time and is not limited to certain kinds of relationships (e.g., parental authority as in adolescence, or one's spouse in marriage). In spite of modern man's moral relativism and supposed sophistication, he still wrestles desperately with the consequences of sin. And he needs the ministrations of the Church at this point whether he is aware of it or not.

IS SIN A SEMANTIC PROBLEM?

. . . the vocabulary of religion and of modern science differ markedly, though their meanings are essentially the same. The religious vocabulary seems dignified but archaic; our scientific vocabulary, persuasive but barbaric. "His Id and super-ego have not learned to cooperate," writes the modern mental hygienist; "The flesh lusteth contrary to the spirit, and the spirit to the flesh," writes Saint Paul. "Feelings of guilt suggest poor personality teamwork," says a twentieth century specialist; "Purify your hearts, ye double-minded," exhorts St. James. "The capacity of the ego to ward off anxiety is enlarged if the ego has considerable affection for his fellows and a positive goal to help them." Correspondingly, St. James writes, "Perfect love casteth out fear." Conscience is astonishingly universal, and is by no means a product of the Christian tradition, certainly not of Puritanism. In all religions we find sin, contrition, and appeal for forgiveness playing a prominent part.[3]

In an attempt to be purely scientific, psychologists, sociologists, and anthropologists have felt it necessary to try very hard to remain morally neutral. Objectivity is the watchword of the scientific method. Yet, embarrassingly enough, on every hand, the practitioners and clinicians in the applied branches of these disciplines are confronted daily with the facts of life: that morality and values are data to be accounted for. The school psychologist must deal with the truant and determine whether or not a violator or "problem child" can still be contained within the group. The psychiatrist is called upon to help determine responsibility in sanity hearings in court.[4] To a theologian this looks like he is determining the defendant's capacity to "sin." And the anthropologist is as disturbed as the next person when he discovers his son has become a

[3] Gordon W. Allport, *The Individual and His Religion* (New York: The Macmillan Company, 1953), pp. 86-88.

[4] *See* Henry A. Davidson's article, "Criminal Responsibility: The Quest for a Formula," in *Psychiatry and the Law*, edited by Paul H. Hoch and Joseph Zubin (New York: Grune and Stratton, 1955), Chapter 5.

homosexual or his daughter is forced to drop out of high school because she is pregnant out of wedlock. Can the behavioral scientists study
man fully and omit this dimension? A superficial glance at the subject indexes of behavioral science books dealing with personality shows
many references to "guilt" and "repression," but they very seldom use
the term "sin."

In his book on *The Psychology of Religion*, Grensted states that "Sin,
as rightly defined, is not a psychological but a theological term. . . . Such
a definition involves metaphysical assumptions about man and God which
lie outside the proper field of psychology and, indeed, of science in general." [5] Professor Mowrer stirred up a flurry of comment from his col-
leagues with an article addressed to psychologists suggesting that not
only the concept of sin but the very term itself should not be avoided.

> For several decades we psychologists looked upon the whole matter of
> sin and moral accountability as a great incubus and acclaimed our lib-
> eration from it as epoch-making. But at length we have discovered that
> to be "free" in this sense; i.e., to have the excuse of being "sick" rather
> than *sinful*, is to court the danger of also becoming *lost*. . . . In becom-
> ing amoral, ethically neutral, and "free," we have cut the very roots of
> our being; lost our deepest sense of self-hood and identity . . . we have
> become suddenly aware, once again, of the problem of *values* and of their
> centrality in the human enterprise.[6]

It is beyond the scope of this discussion to settle this argument, but sufficient to indicate an area needing further research.

Not only is sin a tragic reality, but its inevitable consequence, guilt,
causes untold suffering. If it is not handled therapeutically (the Church
would say redemptively), guilt festers within the psyche and may finally
sink into the unconscious where it continues to cripple and immobilize
the person. Later, the person may not be able to identify the specific
sin or source of his guilt, and a vague, generalized feeling of anxiety
plagues him. We have almost as much semantic difficulty with "guilt"
as with "sin." We must differentiate between real guilt that is appropriate
to the sin, and neurotic "guilt feelings" or a sense of shame that is

[5] L. W. Grensted, *The Psychology of Religion* (New York: Oxford University Press,
1952), pp. 87-88.

[6] O. Hobart Mowrer, " 'Sin', The Lesser of Two Evils," *The American Psychologist*,
Vol. 15, No. 5, May, 1960, pp. 303-04.

See also Thomas S. Szasz's article, "The Myth of Mental Illness," *The American
Psychologist*, Vol. 15, No. 2, February 1960, pp. 113-18. The author feels there is a
place for values, choice, and responsibility. "While it is generally accepted that
mental illness has something to do with man's social (or interpersonal) relations, it
is paradoxically maintained that problems of values (that is, of ethics) do not arise
in this process. . . . My aim is . . . to suggest that the phenomena now called
mental illnesses be looked at afresh and more simply, . . . that they be regarded as
the expression of man's struggle with the problem of *how* he should live." Pp. 116-17.

distorted. When the Church has failed to speak clearly and helpfully in the field of ethics, or when unhealthy fads of puritan scrupulosity govern social mores, we have the situation of which Jesus spoke when he said that the Pharisees bound burdens on the people "too heavy to bear," or that if the blind lead the blind both will fall into the ditch.

> The "fields of association" which the word "guilt" can conjure up are indeed so different that it is no wonder that they can provoke perplexities which amount to mutual incomprehension. To the theologian—as well as the moralist and the lawyer—the word will at once suggest something reprehensible and blameworthy: indeed unpardonable except on strict conditions of repentance and amendment. To the psychologist it will suggest more often a pitiable affliction, probably a delusion; a symptom of a disorder which causes intense suffering, inhibits life and joy in living, and which calls for as much sympathetic understanding and as little reproach as does physical sickness. Although the psychologist will not usually deny that there is such a thing as real culpability, calling for amendment and the sanctions of society, the attitudes towards guilt of the theologian, the moralist and the lawyer will often seem to him quite inhuman and immature; while to them, the attitude of the psychologist will often seem unrealistic, amoral, anarchic, perhaps dangerously sentimental. To this a Christian may be inclined to add that the psychologist's attitude betrays a deplorably frivolous attitude to sin and to its terrible consequences in time and eternity; a view which may only confirm the suspicion of some psychologists that religious teachings are compounded of ignorant fears which are a menace to public health and individual happiness. Each party may become so impatient with the other, that it does not occur to either to ask if they are talking about the same thing.[7]

Surely sin and guilt are more than out-moded forms of speech. The problem is not semantical; both the words and all they imply are as applicable to men today as in the days of the patriarchs of Israel or during the times of Jesus' walk among men. And the beginning point is the same as then; man must begin by admitting the obvious, that he has sinned and fallen short of the glory God had intended for him. Modern psychology is convinced that repression of guilt, avoidance of the problem created by what the Church calls sin, is most harmful to the person's mental health and no solution to the problem at all.

Psychoanalysis, psychiatry of other schools, and counseling in general are agreed that catharsis, frank admission of one's problem, is the most helpful beginning for the client. All must be done to provide an atmosphere conducive to this difficult, and sometimes heart-breaking, task. If the client comes to the psychiatrist and is able to say, "I have a terrible

---

[7] Victor White, "Guilt: Theological and Psychological," in *Christian Essays in Psychiatry,* edited by Philip Mairet (New York: Philosophical Library, 1956), pp. 155-56.

See also James A. Pike's *Beyond Anxiety,* Chapters 3 and 4 on the subject of "Guilt" (New York: Charles Scribner's Sons, 1953).

problem that I've been too ashamed of to tell anyone before; but I'd like to get it off my chest and change my life," the treatment is off to a good start. This brings us to the phase of the treatment the Church has provided for centuries, and the priests of Israel for centuries before that. It is the confession of the repentant heart. It is typified by the words of the Prodigal Son, "Father, I have sinned against heaven and before you; I am no longer worthy to be called your son." [8]

CONFESSION, THE PREREQUISITE FOR COMMUNION

What is Confession?

Answer. Confession consists of two parts: the one is, that we confess our sins; the other, that we receive absolution or forgiveness through the pastor as of God himself, in no wise doubting, but firmly believing that our sins are thus forgiven before God in heaven.

What sins ought we to confess?

Answer. In the presence of God we should acknowledge ourselves guilty of all manner of sins, even of those which we do not ourselves perceive; as we do in the Lord's Prayer. But in the presence of the pastor we should confess those sins alone of which we have knowledge and which we feel in our hearts.

Which are these?

Answer. Here reflect in your condition, according to the Ten Commandments, namely: Whether you are a father or mother, a son or daughter, a master or mistress, a man-servant or maid-servant—whether you have been disobedient, unfaithful, slothful, whether you have injured any one by words or actions, whether you have stolen, neglected, or wasted aught, or done other evil.

Please show me a short way to confess.

Answer. You should speak to the confessor thus: Reverend and dear sir, I beseech you to hear my confession, and to announce to me forgiveness for God's sake.[9]

The above quotation from *The Small Catechism of Luther* and the following quotation from the Augsburg Confession should indicate that confession was considered essential after, as well as before, the Reformation.

Confession in our churches is not abolished; for it is not usual to give the Body of the Lord, except to them that have been previously exam-

---

[8] *Luke* 15:21.
[9] *The Book of Concord,* edited by Henry Eyster Jacobs (Philadelphia: The United Lutheran Publication House, 1911), pp. 371-72.

ined and absolved. . . . Our people are taught that they should highly prize the absolution, as being the voice of God, and pronounced by His command. The power of the Keys is commended, and we show what great consolation it brings to anxious consciences; that God requires faith to believe such absolution as a voice sounding from Heaven, and that such faith in Christ truly obtains and receives the forgiveness of sins.[10]

It is a problem in Church history to explain why confession has been toned down. One has the uncomfortable feeling that much of the motivation lies in party loyalties, in the momentum of pendulum swings to counteract previous errors (sometimes throwing the baby out with the bath water), cultural influences such as secularism and materialism minimizing spiritual factors and practices, philosophical trends such as naturalism, determinism, and the therapeutic work of psychiatric and psychological counselors who have filled the void left by the Church's neglect of the ministry of confession and absolution.

The trend has gone something like this: private, individual confession gave way to a service of public, general confession such as would be held on the day before the administration of the Sacrament. Since in American culture with its five-day work week, Saturday became not only a day off from work but a day for family and recreational activities; it seemed impossible to bring people together for such a service of preparation the day before Communion. An alternative form was made available when the confession occurs immediately before the Service of the day. Meanwhile, in some groups, an attempt was made to preserve the personal relationship between pastor and communicant, to leave the opportunity for confession routinely open. The author recalls from his childhood in a rural Norwegian Lutheran parish that the parishioners who intended to receive Holy Communion would go up front into the sacristy and "register" with the pastor. They would sign the parish Communion record book, and, supposedly, if they had some special burden on their hearts, would have the opportunity to confess it to the pastor at that time. Since the length of stay (beyond the bare minimum of signing one's name and receiving a brief blessing from the pastor) might be noticed and interpreted by others in the congregation, there is the possibility that this was fairly routine. However, at least the opportunity was formally made available and the idea of the necessity of special

---

[10] *Ibid.*, page 52.

See Max Thurian's *Confession* (translated from the French by Edwin Hudson), (London: SCM Press Ltd., 1958), Chapter 1, "Protestant Criticism of the Sacrament of Penance," and Chapter 5, "Confession and Psychoanalysis," for a discussion of both Luther's and Calvin's views.

See also Fulton J. Sheen's *Peace of Soul* (New York: Permabooks Edition, 1954, first published in 1949 by McGraw-Hill), Chapter 7, "Psychoanalysis and Confession," for a strong apologetic for the validity and functionalism of confession.

preparation through confession was emphasized. Another rubric intended to intensify confession and absolution was the laying on of hands as the communicants came forward to the Altar to receive the absolution. Gradually, under the pressure of modern efficiency, crowded time schedules, and growing attendances in large city and suburban churches, the Service has been abbreviated almost to *Readers' Digest* dimensions. The *Gloria in Excelsis* and other parts are often omitted on Communion Sunday, and even the brief form for confession may be shortened. A general atmosphere of haste and expediency is sensed by the people, and attention is focused on the mechanics of efficient ushering so that the church may be cleared before the next service is scheduled to begin. Thus, several hundred are communed in about forty-five minutes. The automobile and the traffic problem in the parking lots have no small influence upon the whole arrangement. Meanwhile, what is left of the personal relationship between penitent and confessor is a stack of communion attendance cards which the secretary enters in the church register on Monday.

Considering how many people choose a clergyman for help with personal problems, it certainly behooves the pastor to know what resources he has at hand and how to use them as dynamically as possible.[11] It would be ironical if the people in need were seeking out the confessor in great numbers at the same time as he was minimizing and abrogating his own unique function.

There seems to be more than a symbolic or mythical need for the "three fathers." The first, the natural and physical father is taken for granted by everyone. The "godfather," or as the Germans say, *taufvater* (baptism father), has already been referred to in our chapter on Baptism as the sponsor who will step in and be a father figure in the case of the death or disability of the natural father. He represents society's social and protective responsibility for the child. The third is the "father confessor" (German *beichtvater*) who, as the spiritual father and representative of the Church, guides the straying child back to the right path again, who

---

[11] A recent survey listed the following breakdown concerning "Source of Help Used by People Who Have Sought Professional Help for a Personal Problem": (a brief summary in part)

Clergymen	42%
Doctor	29%
Psychiatrist	18%
(including psychologists in clinics)	
Lawyer	6%

Americans View Their Mental Health, A Nationwide Survey, by Gerald Gurin, Joseph Veroff, and Sheila Feld (New York: Basic Books, Inc., Publishers, 1960), p. 307. *See* entire Chapter 10, "People Who Have Gone for Help."

See also David Belgum, *Why Did It Happen To Me?* Chapter 3, "Communion and Cure" (Minneapolis: Augsburg Publishing House, 1960).

restores him to the "state of grace." Thus man is cared for physically, socially, and religiously.

A paranoid patient or a parishioner with a pathologically scrupulous conscience cannot make a valid confession, but must first be restored to a healthy sense of reality before he can make meaningful statements of repentance. It is not only unnecessary, it is inappropriate for a midwestern farmer who has never been outside his own state to confess sole responsibility for the Korean War; nor is he to be credited with the achievements of Napoleon. Only after he has been helped to know who he *really* is and what wrong he has *really* done can he make a meaningful confession to the hospital chaplain or his home pastor. For this real condition of sin or these real acts of sin he can usefully receive absolution. For the conflicts, estrangements, hostilities, and tragedies that originally led to his delusions and hallucinations, for these offenses and broken relationships the Church has a truly curative therapy in the Holy Communion. And confession is the door to this treasure house of blessing.

SACRAMENTAL GRACE AND SUPPORTIVE POWER

Mental hygienists speak not only of cathartic therapy but also of supportive therapy. Providing a person with false teeth may be an excellent remedy even though in a technical sense it may not be called a "cure." Fortunately, we do not have to choose between surgery and braces. There are many times when both are used. As much of the diseased tissue is rooted out as possible and then crutches or other supports aid the person to keep his balance and supplement his weakened condition. So in mental or spiritual therapy. The soul is cleansed by the catharsis of confession, but still the traumatized psyche needs guidance, encouragement, "ego-support," and other stabilizing positive measures.

Nothing is more supportive than the doctrine of Grace—that God will infuse His very own power into a person's life without any merit or deserving of his own. We have in the words of administration of Holy Communion the most positive power of religion concentrated in one place and in one ceremony. It is highlighted in every way. The Elements of Bread and Wine are consecrated at the Altar. The Presence of Christ is highlighted in the Body and the Blood. There is a wholesome balance between objectivity (Church doctrine and the group) and subjectivity (mystical union with Christ in the Sacrament). The *Sanctus* is full of power and majesty—"Heaven and earth are full of thy glory; Hosanna in the highest." And the *Nunc Dimittis* is full of positive reassurance and thanksgiving—"Lord, now lettest thou thy servant depart in peace according to thy word; for mine eyes have seen thy salvation which thou hast prepared before the face of all people." Many sense a special personal meaning in the Benediction when it is pronounced at the close of the Holy Communion.

Now is the time for rejoicing. If forgiveness is taken seriously, all sin is now in the past. If God has accepted man through the Sacrament, now man can also accept himself and lift up his head again. And here is the sad fact, that many do not take such a new view of themselves; they leave the church as downcast and depressed as when they came in. Whence this heresy? Whence this lack of joy at the effects of the Gospel proclamation? Listen to Saint Paul. "Therefore, if any one is in Christ, he is a new creation; the old has passed away, behold, the new has come." [12] ". . . be transformed by the renewal of your mind, that you may prove what is the will of God, what is good and acceptable and perfect." [13] Or listen to the joyous ending of our Lord's parable of the Prodigal Son.

> But the father said to his servants, "Bring quickly the best robe, and put it on him; and put a ring on his hand, and shoes on his feet; and bring the fatted calf and kill it, and let us eat and make merry; for this my son was dead, and is alive again; he was lost, and is found." And they began to make merry.[14]

AN OCCASION FOR PASTORAL CARE AND EVANGELISM

There could hardly be any topic that would more directly lead to pastoral and soul care conversation than a discussion of Holy Communion whether in group study or in individual conversation. Seward Hiltner has helpfully used the term "precounseling" to refer to efforts that will pave the way for soul-searching, that will help a person face himself and his problems in a way which he otherwise might have avoided. Consider the "lapsed member"—the one who is on probation because he has not communed, attended, or contributed for a year or more. Indeed! there should be criteria for active, bona fide membership. Two motives prompt the investigation of a lapsed member or one who is headed in that direction. First, there should be an effort to rekindle his

---

[12] *II Corinthians* 5:17.

[13] *Romans* 12:2.

See David Belgum, *Guilt: Where Psychology and Religion Meet,* Chapter 2, "The Triad of Morality" and Chapter 7, "A Functional Confessional" (Englewood Cliffs, New Jersey: Prentice-Hall, Inc., 1962). Here the author discusses the significance of follow-up work with the penitent after the absolution has been pronounced. Some traditions speak of this as "growth in grace," "sanctification," or the necessity to avoid "backsliding." Roman Catholics refer to it as the third part of Penance: "satisfaction."

[14] *Luke* 15:22-24.

zeal; secondly, if he has definitely turned his back on Word and Sacraments, this decision and action on his part should be reflected in the formal membership list. If this practice were generally adhered to, church statistics would be more honest and dependable.

The lapsed or inactive member can be approached in several ways. "After all, if all our members don't get behind the program, our church will not go forward." "Considering the building drive we're in and all the good our church is doing in the community with the young people, I'm sure we can count on your support." "The Church needs you as much as you need the Church." (One pastor even offered the bribe of a committee chairmanship if the member would reconsider and "come back.")

Another approach would be to ask the person how else he would solve the problems that arise in his life as a result of sin and failure. Where will he turn in times of crisis and tragedy? This can be broached without any sense of "holier-than-thou" judgment, but as the inevitable and universal problem that all of us face—the need for continuing cure for the malady of sin. The pastor would not want to make this a polemical argument, but, if the rationale of this chapter is sound, it could serve as a starting point for discussion. If he does not want to reactivate his spiritual life in the Church for this basic reason, there is little value in appealing to him on the basis of "togetherness," "a fine thing to do for the children," or, "everyone really ought to belong to some church." Anyone who does not need forgiveness of sins should not belong to a church. Jesus said the sick need a physician, not the well. Through Holy Communion the Great Physician is offering therapy to those who know themselves to be in need of it.

The use of the sermon for deepening the people's appreciation of, and full participation in, Holy Communion should be exploited. Parts of the Communion liturgy could well serve as topical texts from time to time (indeed some of them do come from the regular pericope series). It would be hard to exhaust this topic. And it needs reinterpretation and application so as not to become stale, routine, and shop-worn. The author found the *Agnus Dei* from the Communion Service a fruitful theme for a mid-week Lenten series, and the same could be said for the Words of Institution, the Proper Prefaces, and parts of the Order for Public Confession such as Psalm 51 or The Exhortation. An adult Bible class could trace the biblical origins of the various parts of the liturgy for Communion and study those passages of Scripture in their larger context. The doctrinal implications (or inferences) would be stimulating for the more academic-minded groups. The music, art, and symbolism that have grown up in connection with the Eucharist would be a rewarding study for those so inclined. Again, we can only say, it would not be easy to exhaust the riches and wonder of this Sacrament nor to over-emphasize its value for the personal devotional life of the believer. In either the out-

ward or inward thrust of evangelism as it is understood today, Holy
Communion is both an opportunity and a great resource. In it are merged
the Word of life and the Bread of life.

Every pastor knows what a comfort Communion is to the sick and the
shut-in. As a seventy-eight year old parishioner, who had been unable
to attend church for over a dozen years, said, "It is wonderful that when
I cannot go to the church, the church can come to me." She always had
a clean cloth on a little table beside her chair and a candle "like in church"
when the pastor would come with the Sacrament. One sensed that this
was in a very real sense a "home altar." Such shut-ins, the aged, the
arthritic, and so forth, should have as frequent opportunity to receive
the Sacrament as those who are more fortunate—in short, as often as it
is offered in the church. It is outside the scope of this discussion to go
into detail about the mechanics of the administration, but it should be
done with such dignity and reverence as is found in the church. In the
hospital, a nurse will be glad to see that curtains are drawn and the
Service is not interrupted.[15] The attitude of the pastor toward the need
of the sick and shut-in to have Holy Communion made available to them
would be a good barometer of his view of the ministry.

PRACTICAL MATTERS

Americans are pragmatists and seemingly becoming more
so with each passing year. Yet, if one has properly "put first things
first," if one is governed by principle rather than by expediency, then
there is a place for consideration of practical matters. A clumsy and unnecessarily tedious administration of the Sacrament does not enhace its
piety. Courteous and unostentatious ushering can facilitate the service of
worship and reduce the distractions of confusion. When things are done
in good order, people are more likely to focus their attention on the important matters and not to be drawn to adiaphora and mechanics.

There are things that can legitimately be omitted to reduce the length
of a Communion with a large attendance. The rubrics indicate that some
hymns are optional. Announcements, to say the very least, could be
eliminated. If done properly, the continuous line at the Altar Rail can save
much time without giving the appearance of rushing people. It is becoming more common and acceptable to say the blessing after all have communed rather than after each "Table" has communed. This naturally
applies to the liturgical tradition and not to the Reformed churches in

---

[15] For a thorough and practical discussion of Communion in the hospital see
Granger Westberg's *Nurse, Patient and Pastor* (Rock Island, Illinois: Augustana Book
Concern).

which it is the practice to receive the Elements in the pews, the administration being conducted by Deacons.

Faulty church architecture is frequently to blame. Sometimes the large church seating a thousand has provision for an even dozen at the Altar Rail, which is cramped into a tiny box of a Chancel. It was evidently not anticipated that many would be using it, for there is often better provision for "traffic" in the social kitchen serving area than at the Altar. Thus church architecture is a good index of what the parish *actually* believes about its own faith and life.

The circular or octagonal church shape with the pews facing the Altar from all sides also provides a long Altar Rail and thereby facilitates the administration process. At any rate, provision for celebrating the Sacrament should not be at the bottom of the architect's list as "other details to check." The Reformed Churches in which members receive Communion in their pews do not face this problem.

The spacing of services is another practical matter. If they are spaced too close together, it becomes practically impossible to celebrate the Sacrament as a regular (let us say monthly) matter of course. It is difficult to see how "rushing" can be avoided if they are spaced less than an hour and a half apart. There are two reasons why Roman Catholic churches can begin a Mass each hour Sunday morning. First, Confession has been taken care of the day before; second, since the Eucharist is celebrated every Sunday, not everyone in the parish receives it at the same time (many who "hear Mass" do not receive Communion on a given Sunday).

Again, record keeping is important for many of the same reasons as were given for accurate Baptism records; i.e., to keep track of individual members. Jesus said he knew his own sheep by name, and so should the Church. It is as important to know the communing membership as it is to know the baptized and confirmed membership roll accurately.

We have not sketched out every detail, but have rather attempted to set forth general guide lines and perspectives whereby we may see how Holy Communion is related to the general and particular needs of man, as well as the attitude that pastor and people should have toward it in the life and practice of the Church. Let us remember the words of our Blessed Lord when he said,

> . . . Take, eat; this is my Body, which is given for you; this do in remembrance of me. . . .

> . . . Drink ye all of it; this cup is the New Testament in my Blood, which is shed for you, and for many, for the remission of sins; this do, as oft as ye drink it, in remembrance of me.[16]

[16] From the Words of Institution sometimes referred to as "the Canon of the Mass."

CHAPTER 11

BURIAL

AND THE FUNCTION

OF THE FUNERAL

Lord, let me know mine end, and the number of my days; that I may be certified how long I have to live. Behold, thou hast made my days as it were a span long, and mine age is even as nothing in respect of thee; and verily every man living is altogether vanity.[1]

The fact that he (man) is creature is expressed in the term finitude. The awareness of it is expressed in the term anxiety. Anxiety is the awareness of finitude. Man comes from nothing and goes to nothing. He always lives in the conscious or unconscious anxiety of having to die. Non-being is present in every moment of his being. Suffering, accidents, disease, loss of relations to nature and man, loneliness, insecurity, weakness, and error are always with him. Finally, the threat of having to die will become the reality of death.[2]

Death is the last great crisis man has to face, and no one escapes it. Again we find that societies around the globe and throughout history have provided many aids for their members in the forms of rites and ceremonies to help them face the fact of death. As such, the Christian funeral has a long and honorable history. Whether one is contemplating his own death or that of a loved one, there is need for strengthening support. According to Tillich, cited above, there is an inevitable anxiety connected with death for which no amount of psychotherapy is adequate. The Church has affirmed that through its teachings regarding salvation and the Resurrection there is hope to rise above this morbid anxiety. The ministry of the Church in

[1] *Psalm* 39:4-5 according to the version used in the *Book of Common Prayer*, p. 324.
[2] Paul Tillich, "The Theology of Pastoral Care," *Pastoral Psychology*, Vol. 10, October, 1959, p. 23.

connection with death is designed to support man in his last great crisis and to heal and comfort those left behind in bereavement.

THE CRISIS OF DYING AND THE WORK OF GRIEVING

Death comes in a hundred ways and more. Some die suddenly in battle, others die suddenly in industrial or automobile accidents. People die while swimming on their summer vacations or while engaged in other wholesome recreation. Others invite death through hazardous vocations such as auto racing or hair-raising circus feats. But by far the most of us will very likely die in a hospital bed with oxygen tubes, intravenous tubes for blood transfusions or feeding, amidst professional strangers highly skilled in combating death. There will be medications to reduce the pain of disease and mechanical devices to aid our failing organs. Death may come in infancy, youth, the prime of life, or old age. There is never a time when it should surprise us, and yet never a "right" time for dying. Whenever it comes it is a crisis, if only for a fleeting moment.

The Church can and should do much to prepare people for this last great "rite of passage"; a passage from this life to the next.[3] Here sermons, group discussions, and stimulating reading matter can be employed.[4] If the parishioners are to be educated in their attitude toward death by modern secular standards, they will be ill prepared indeed for the crisis. A sensate culture tries by din and activisim to avoid such a basic issue and prefers to deal with trivialities. Oh, the paperback trash at the newsstand will deal with murder and violence, sadism and torture, but it is still a diversion and fictional entertainment, not a coming to grips with the issue.

When there is some warning of impending death, the pastor is usually involved. He will have called on the person during his illness in the hospital or at home. There may have been deep personal discussions about the patient's impending death, private administration of Holy Communion, and some preparation on the part of the family for what they expect will soon happen. During these weeks or days, all concerned have

[3] The author's *His Death and Ours* (Minneapolis: Augsburg Publishing House, 1958), is aimed at preparation of parishioners in a devotional-psychological way for both death and bereavement so they can better face it when it comes.

[4] Westminster Press has two excellent short works suitable for the layman's understanding: *And Peace at the Last*, by Russell L. Dicks and Thomas S. Kepler (1953), and *Life, Death, and Destiny* by Roger L. Shinn (1957). Others of this type should be in the parish library.

See also How to Face Death, by Cecil Clark, an Anglican hospital chaplain in London, The Faith Press Ltd., 7 Tufton Street, London, S. W. 1, 1958.

an opportunity to draw upon many resources: Scripture, doctrines of the Church, pastoral care, Holy Communion, the fellowship of family and friends, chances to set one's affairs in order, and so on.

Ideally, the following verses from Saint Paul will be typical of the Scripture passages that will be personally suited to the comfort of the dying believer:

> I am now ready to be offered, and the time of departure is at hand. I have fought a good fight, I have finished my course, I have kept the faith; henceforth there is laid up for me a crown of righteousness, which the Lord, the righteous Judge, shall give me at that day; and not to me only, but unto all them also that love his appearing. (*II Timothy* 4:6-8)

> For God has not destined us for wrath, but to obtain salvation through our Lord Jesus Christ, who died for us so that whether we wake or sleep we might live with him. Therefore encourage one another and build one another up, just as you are doing. (*I Thessalonians* 5:8-10)

These are the things one has said, affirmed, and repeated in the church all along; if they have not been mere lip service, they should now be a pillar of strength and comfort as one looks death squarely in the face.

Contrary to the impression left by romantic novels concerning death-bed scenes, death is not frequently dramatic. Nature provides an anaesthetic for pain and suffering; and often the patient is only partially aware of his surroundings, only able to give partial attention to his visitors. He may not be able to communicate his inner thoughts coherently, and relatives may be disappointed that he, "who was always such a spiritual man," does not rise up from his pillow and give some stirring testimony of faith. Meanwhile, the dying person is preoccupied with getting a drink of water or finding a more comfortable position in the bed or chair so he can breath more easily. More understanding and empathy are needed at this point by all concerned.

Now the familiar expressions will be easier to follow: well-known passages of Scripture, frequently used calls to worship, invocations, favorite Psalms, beloved hymn verses, the Benediction, etc. All concerned should try to assess the person's capacity to discuss new ideas or follow more complicated paths of thinking. Naturally, each dying person is unique, and some will be clear headed almost to the end. Since the sense of hearing is the last (supposedly) to leave the person, we will continue to speak and act in his presence as though he were aware of us—not whisper "secrets" in the room as though he were an inanimate object. Dying persons should still be treated as *persons*. There can be both extremes—from the person reconciled to God in the eleventh hour like the dying thief on the cross beside Jesus, to the old saint who has been a Christian and consciously a child of God all her life.

Would it not be tragic if the dying person, weak and resigned to his death, should be thinking with Simeon, "Lord, now lettest thou thy servant depart in *peace* . . . ;" and his relatives, medical attendants, and pastor were acting in a great rush and panic conveying anything but peace? No wonder "The Last Rites" are a comfort to many because they provide something tangible and specific to be done in this anxious time. One form used in Protestantism may be accompanied by the laying on of hands, sign of the cross, or other symbols:

Depart, O Christian soul, out of this world,
  In the Name of God the Father Almighty who created thee.
  In the Name of Jesus Christ who redeemed thee.
  In the Name of the Holy Ghost who sanctifieth thee.
May thy rest be this day in peace, and thy dwelling place in the Paradise
  of God.[5]

We come to the second part of this section, "the work of grieving." There comes a time when the greater need is felt by the bereaved than by the dying person. The dying person can experience with the Christ of Easter, "The strife is o'er, the battle done; Now is the Victor's triumph won; Now be the song of praise begun, Alleluia!" But what of those who remain to fight the long and lonely battle with grief? They must now be cared for.

The writer cannot vouch for the origin of the following story, but he believes he first heard Malcolm Ballinger, Chaplain of University of Michigan Hospital, tell it.

A middle-aged railroad switchman and his wife lived near the tracks within sight of his usual place for reporting to work. One morning as he was walking to work, his wife waved to him from the back door of their apartment and was horrified to see him slip on the icy tracks, fall under a moving box car and be cut nearly in two. First there was the shock of it all, then the sound of police and ambulance sirens, and, finally, Andy's body was removed from the scene. Mrs. Jones is dazed by it all; she does not know what to do with herself. A few neighbor ladies take her back to her apartment over the corner grocery story. After they have poured her a cup of coffee, she sits down and begins to speak.

"I can't believe it! Just this morning we were in this very kitchen to-gether. Andy got up first as he always did and put on the coffee before he shaved. Then I got up and made pancakes—we always had pancakes on Friday. We had another cup of coffee, and I kissed Andy goodbye. I told him to be careful because it was slippery. I waved to him as he crossed the tracks. When I saw him fall, I screamed, 'No! It can't be—It's Andy!' I can't believe it!" She breaks down weeping.

[5] *The Book of Common Prayer*, p. 319.

Then a relative from across town arrives at the apartment, and Mrs. Jones tells about it again between sobs.

"I can't believe it! Just this morning we were together in this very apartment. It was like any other morning. Andy got up first as he always did and put the coffee on. Then I made pancakes while he shaved . . . etc., etc."

People come and go during the day. The undertaker phones to make some arrangements. The pastor will have called on her as soon as he hears of the accident. The foreman from the railroad crew stops by to offer his sympathy and say that Andy had always been a good worker and friend. And each time she repeats herself as she goes over the events surrounding her husband's death.

Many who are closest to the scene will begin to be alarmed for Mrs. Jones' welfare. They will say, "It's too much for her; she's got to stop thinking about this awful thing or she'll drive herself nuts." Sympathetically, they try to take the burden from her, to get her to talk about something more pleasant, to lie down and take a rest, to take a couple of aspirin, etc. Such sympathy is well meant; but there is no short-cut through the painful and arduous work of grief. It is rightly referred to by many as grief *work.* There will also be suggestions to "get away from it all." "Why don't you go visit your sister in California? We'll have a real estate agent sell the place for you, and when you come back, you can move into a nice little apartment and you can start life all over again." Any of these approaches dodges the issues and hinders the bereaved person in his efforts to deal constructively with reality. They are not sound theologically nor from a mental health point of view. Death is a hard, cold fact that must be faced and lived through honestly, not avoided through a feigned stoicism.

There is now much literature on grief work and bereavement both in psychiatric and pastoral care fields.[6] The tragic Coconut Grove night club fire in Boston provided observers opportunity to compare reactions of many people under varied conditions in their respective bereavements. The situation was almost like the biblical reference to the end time when two will be grinding at the mill and one will be taken, but the other left; two will be in the same bed, the one taken, the other left. So it was that night when many hundred died in flames. Sometimes it was the boyfriend who was left, or the husband who died. The partner dealt with the bereavement from a hospital bed with varying degrees of burns and injury. Those who could talk about the deceased, who could cry and express themselves as fully as possible seemed to make the best recovery

---

[6] *See* Edgar N. Jackson's *Understanding Grief* (New York: Abingdon Press, 1957), for a good summary of the research in this field and helpful practical applications to the role of the minister in this connection.

and adjustment; whereas, those who bottled up their feelings, refused to face the harsh and cruel facts, those who repressed it or ignored it made poor adjustments, took longer to recover from their burns, or, in extreme cases, actually had a psychotic break with reality.[7]

If we are agreed that grief work needs to be done, we need now to turn to the opportunities that are open to the pastor to facilitate such a process.

PASTORAL OPPORTUNITIES TO BRING HEALING AND HOPE

One of the most important principles for the pastor to follow in aiding the bereavement process is to allow full expression of grief. Do not stifle this catharsis of tears. Minutes of tears and honest grief in the beginning may be worth hours and weeks of psychotherapy years later. Getting back to the story of Mrs. Jones, the widow of the railroad switchman; she needs to tell her story over and over again until she believes it. Note how she usually begins and ends her account, "I can't believe it!" Also, she must accept the fact that *all* of her husband is dead—that part that went to family reunions, that part that celebrated Christmas each year, that part that earned the income, yes, and even that part that got up first every morning and made the coffee before breakfast. She may have to go back in her mind's eye and relive many associations and memories of her dead husband. She must become reconciled to the past before she can launch into the future creatively and constructively. She may tell her pastor many of her recollections concerning Andy—how just last month all the children (and the four grandchildren) came to their house for Andy's fiftieth birthday party, how wonderful their silver wedding anniversary had been a few years back, how they had decided (somewhat against Mrs. Jones' wishes, "but then Andy could be stubborn at times") to buy this corner building with the apartment upstairs and the rental income from the store downstairs, how they had met and married, and all about their early plans and hopes and later disappointments.

The parish pastor ought to plan routinely to make a few casual calls on the bereaved during the early weeks after the funeral. If his schedule is crowded, he has to evaluate the priority of his various activities. If the parish is too large, there is need for more staff so that such an essential ministry as this to the bereaved will not have to suffer by default.

---

[7] A psychiatrist, Erich Lindemann, then of Massachusetts General Hospital, who worked with these cases, is a pioneer researcher in the problem of grief reactions.

He will not be needed to the same extent in every case, but he should make himself available.

Devotions and informal worship are suitable and appreciated in general in the home and with the family perhaps at the funeral parlor after the visitors and friends have left for the evening. Most service books have more materials than are needed for the funeral service itself.

Funeral sermons have frequently not received as careful preparation as the Sunday morning sermon. One pastor vainly tried to comfort the mourners in the case of a suicide by referring to the fact that the man had been drunk at the time and therefore not really responsible. Another preacher gave vague generalizations about the pride of life and how some seem to think that honor and fame in this world was all that counted. He actually said, "Some think the greatest achievement is to get their name in the papers." The seventeen-year-old boy in the casket had shot himself and it was a completely open question whether it had been accidental or on purpose, and the incident *had been in the newspaper.* The latter sermon could as well have been given as a moral lecture most anywhere and any time; the former sermon was trying too hard to make it personal and do all the grief work, comforting, and so forth during a ten minute address.

Surely if the pastor has done his duty on a personal basis before the funeral and plans to follow up the situation afterwards with the relatives, the funeral service itself should be filled with the great promises of the Scripture concerning the Resurrection and the destiny of those who die in the faith.

> But we would not have you ignorant, brethren, concerning those who are asleep, that you may not grieve as others do who have no hope. For since we believe that Jesus died and rose again, even so, through Jesus, God will bring with him those who have fallen asleep.[8]

> We are more than conquerors through him that loved us. For I am persuaded, that neither life, nor angels, nor principalities, nor powers, nor things present, nor things to come, nor height, nor depth, nor any other creature, shall be able to separate us from the love of God, which is in Christ Jesus our Lord.[9]

The funeral service itself is a wonderful opportunity to meet the needs of the people while worshipping God "out of the depths." Hymns, responses, all joining in the Lord's Prayer or responsive reading of the Psalms, and so on, should be employed in such a way as to encourage maximum participation of the mourners and those of the congregation

---

[8] *I Thessalonians* 4:13-14.
[9] *Romans* 8:37-39.

who have come to share this experience. If the practice is to stand or kneel for certain parts of the Sunday worship, there is no reason why this service for the Burial of the Dead should be any more passive. It is even more urgent that the participants be involved and express themselves fully. There is no reason why the choir should not rehearse, and the organist be fully familiar with, the musical parts of the funeral liturgy if such are provided.

The setting of the funeral should be the Christian church as naturally as any other service of worship. At least it ought to be the exception to the rule for any member of a Christian congregation to have the funeral service in a commercial funeral parlor chapel. More of this in the last section of this chapter. We shall also discuss pastoral leadership in that connection.

The behavior of the mourners is unfortunately scanned by others to see "how well they took it." Those who seem quite unmoved (more often than not due to heavy repression) are considered to have a strong Christian faith, stoic lack of emotion being in this case a virtue. The widow who weeps during part of the service in the church or who "goes to pieces" at the grave is considered to have failed in her adjustment, to be a weak person or "too high strung." From our discussion of grief work above, we see that the opposite is more likely the case. Contrast our altogether too prevalent concept of "good" funeral behavior with the following instances from Scripture:

> And when all the congregation saw that Aaron was dead, all the house of Israel wept for Aaron thirty days.[10]

> Then Joseph fell on his father's face, and wept over him, and kissed him. And Joseph commanded his servants the physicians to embalm his father. So the physicians embalmed Israel; forty days were required for embalming. And the Egyptians wept for him seventy days.[11]

> Then David said to Joab and to all the people who were with him, "Rend your clothes, and gird on sackcloth, and mourn before Abner." And King David followed the bier. They buried Abner at Hebron; and the king lifted up his voice and wept at the grave of Abner; and all the people wept.[12]

> When Jesus saw her weeping, and the Jews who came with her also weeping, he was deeply moved in spirit and troubled; and he said, "Where have you laid him [Lazarus]?" They said to him, "Lord, come and see." Jesus wept. So the Jews said, "See how he loved him!"[13]

[10] *Numbers* 20:29.
[11] *Genesis* 50:1-3.
[12] *II Samuel* 3:31-33.
[13] *John* 11:33-36.

THE ROLE OF THE LAYMAN IN THE CARE
OF THE BEREAVED

Specialization characterizes our age. Before and after a death in the family, we will have highly trained personnel efficiently carrying out intricate details. The hospital staff including a pathologist for the autopsy, a lawyer to deal with the will and estate, the undertaker, the pastor, are all professional people. By no means all of these have been considered essential until the recent past. Is there still a place for the general layman in the care of the bereaved; the neighbor, the uncle, the friend, the fellow church member?

The writer remembers a parishioner of his who was a sort of self-appointed Deacon in charge of informal help when there was a death in the parish. He was an elderly retired businessman who was still in good health and had a lot of time on his hands. In a case where a widow or widower did not have many close relatives, he would pay a visit and offer his services, ranging from a ride to the cemetery to select a lot for burial, to giving advice on income tax matters. It was a kind of "bear one another's burdens and so fulfill the law of Christ" ministry for which he was well-suited. And the service was usually needed and always appreciated.

Friendly help should be volunteered in such a way that it can be graciously declined if not needed, and in such a way as not to take responsibility entirely away from the bereaved. They need the experience of working with the details of the burial as much as possible because it helps them to accept the reality of the death; but at the same time it is helpful not to have to do this in isolation—to have someone with whom to share feelings and experiences. The more kinds of people there are involved the better. The bereaved might talk over one kind of problem or feeling with a fellow businessman that he would not discuss with his sister "because she'd think it was awfully cold and mercenary." The son who is supposed to be strong for the sake of his bereaved mother may need someone else with whom to share his tears, and hopefully in a Christian congregation, the pastor would not be the *only* one available for expression, compassion, understanding, and support. This would be a tangible way of implementing that phrase in the Third Article of the Apostles' Creed wherein "the Holy Christian Church" is equated with "the Communion of Saints"—a genuine and meaningful fellowship.

The "wake" is associated usually with the Irish Catholic tradition, but the same function, stepping up social interaction, is frequently cared for in other ways. Even though the body is removed from the home, where it used to lie in state for a few days, the family usually spends a couple of evenings and an afternoon at the funeral parlor greeting those who come to express sympathy. This is very fruitful, because different visitors are bound to mention different aspects of the deceased's life and social relations. One will speak about his work, another about his hobbies or how he kept his yard, the picnics they had together, or the favors that were received. Another will ask if there is any way in which he can help— with the children, with meals, with transportation, and so forth.

The Christian congregation should be alert to the needs of people in such times of stress and should have routine plans for helping at time of death. Many churches have a rotating list of women's groups or "circles" which take turns serving a lunch in the church parlors or in the home after the funeral, since many relatives and friends may have traveled some distance. Surely this is an obvious need for hospitality in the Old Testament sense of helping the "widow, the fatherless and the stranger in your midst." Again, this is not done to shield the mourners from the stresses of grief work but to socialize the bereavement process and make it as broad and meaningful as possible. Local customs and traditions, the differences, for example, of rural, urban, and nationalistic cultures, will help to dictate appropriate services and types of help needed.

Recourse may be to community agencies such as homemaker services from a social service agency, visiting nursing care, the obtaining of old age assistance, mother's aid, or direct relief. Where possible, the bereaved should participate as actively as possible in all such decisions and applications, but in their state of shock and depression, they may not be able to think clearly and logically about even quite ordinary matters in the first few days or weeks.

It is a little late to start organizing these services on a congregational level after a crisis occurs. Since we can expect death five or ten or twenty times a year depending upon the size of the congregation, it would seem wiser to have a plan and to train the members to carry it out.

THE FUNERAL AND THE FIELD OF EVANGELISM

Many businesses find that satisfied customers are their best advertising. Physicians and lawyers, who are not allowed to advertise in the newspapers because of their ethical code, rely upon their clients' telling their friends and relatives how much they were helped with their illness or legal problems. Such "unsolicited recommendations" are usually considered trustworthy because the one making them has no vested interest at stake. It is a spontaneous testimony. In a sense this is what also happens when persons find that religious resources and experiences have been very meaningful in their lives. They cannot help but express appreciation and share their gratitude.

In the Gospel accounts we have several records of how someone was so moved or helped that he wanted to share the good news with another. Philip answered the call and passed it along.

> Philip found Nathanael, and said to him, "We have found him of whom Moses in the law and also the prophets wrote, Jesus of Nazareth. . . . Come and see." [14]

When the Samaritan woman by the well found her conversation with Jesus had turned out to be a significant spiritual experience, she shared the discovery with others.

> So the woman left her water jar, and went away into the city, and said to the people, "Come, see a man who told me all that I ever did. Can this be the Christ?" They went out of the city and were coming to him.[15]

Surely, in our churches, if the bereaved have been well cared for, if the funeral sermon has been truly helpful, the parishioners considerate in their concern and compassion, those who are outside the Church will be drawn by the warmth of this fellowship. They may say to themselves, "Here is something I need; here is understanding and help for the really basic issues of life."

We do not wish to reduce the importance of conducting routine campaigns of community census and evangelism visitation; but in regard to the great crises of life from birth and Baptism to death and burial there is a special kind of applicable appeal. Here one sees the doctrines and claims of the Church put into dynamic practice. Here is an appeal or call that plumbs the depths of life and gets under the skin of the superficial agnostic who claims to have intellectual hurdles that keep him out of the fellowship of the Church. Here are experiences that soften up the insensitive materialist. Here is the Church seen in its best light, in the ministry of compassion where no one can deny its relevance. Here is the Church ministering rather than being ministered unto. Here the Church is performing services that no other agency of society can simulate successfully.

Naturally, many who attend the funeral will be bona fide members of other Christian churches. Some friends or relatives may have no church home and are legitimate "prospects" and could be quite naturally called upon later in their homes or could receive some mailing. This is not an appeal to "play to the grandstand." It is a reminder that the "world" watches with special interest and unguarded openness (perhaps mixed with morbid curiosity) at such crucial times as funerals. For some it is

---

[14] *John* 1:45-46.
[15] *John* 4:28-31.

their only contact with the Church and its ministry for years at a time—
until the next death in their family or circle of acquaintances.

UNDERSTANDING THE UNDERTAKER
AND CHURCH POLICY

What is the relationship between the undertaker and the
pastor? It may be one of dignified mutual respect on the part of two professionally trained and accredited men, each with a unique function
to perform. Or one may be subservient to the other. Sometimes there
have been sharp clashes and struggles for prestige. Until recent outbursts
of revolt, the clergy have more often than not adapted to the program
and plans of the mortician, who offers "complete funeral services."

The minister recognizes his subservience when the undertaker hands
him a folded note saying on the outside, "In Appreciation," and, on the
inside, "The family of John Jones has asked us to hand you this hono-
rarium," signed, "Smith Brothers." The implication is clear. The pastor
does church work for which he is paid by the congregation, and, then, on
the side, he does some extra-curricular work as chaplain to the Smith
Brothers Funeral Chapel. The point is even more clear when the family
receives their itemized bill which lists the "minister's fee" along with
limousine service and flower car.

The clergy have many of their own number to blame for this situation.
The less scrupulous have practically "attached" themselves to such
nearby funeral parlors with which they could make convenient connections to supplement their small salaries, and the arrangement has proven
useful to both parties. However, the point is that these "contracts" begin
and usually end as purely private commercial deals and lack the sense
of a ministry of the *Church.*

There are other indications of "who's boss" in the funeral service. Are
all arrangements made, and then as an after-thought, the minister is
"notified" of the time of the burial service? Is the pastor consulted about
where the service is to be held, or has the undertaker already "sold" the
family on the convenience of having it in the funeral parlor's chapel
instead of in the church? What is so different about this worship service
that the congregation will not need the hymnals and service books usually
taken for granted in the pew racks for other services of worship? What
will be done at the grave side? There was a time when churches owned
a special small trowel or little spade for use in the committal service. Now
the funeral director asks the pastor as he walks toward the grave, "What
do you use, soil or flowers?" and hands him rose petals, or a neat, clean
vial of washed, white sand.

Before beginning a self-righteous tirade against the morticians as a class, let us look at what they can do and should do. State law frequently sets standards for embalming and burial. Morticians must be accredited and licensed. There are many routine details with which the pastor would not want to, and should not be, involved. There are paper work and records that must be legally and correctly filed. An item in the obituary column of the daily paper must be submitted on time. The pastor would not want to be bothered with all the phone calls that would result if this item were not correct or on time for the proper publicity of time and place of service or committal. The funeral establishment arranges for umbrellas or awnings in case of rain, procures motorcycle police escort for the auto procession (a must for either a long procession or heavy city traffic), provides calm, poised direction of many details that other people would simply not think about. There are many reasons why clergy and undertakers should and must work together harmoniously rather than merely get mad and make nasty remarks behind each other's backs.

Funeral directors have often lacked a psychological understanding of grief work. They have thought it a great service to spare the mourners as much stress and involvement as possible. The mourners are sometimes seated in overstuffed furniture off to one side out of view of the congregation (in funeral chapels) so that if one of them should show some emotion it would not be noticed by others. Think what this does to limit expressing and sharing grief experience. The music is usually far below the standard of good church music. The extra heavy carpet, the excessive cosmetology that makes many viewers remark, "He never looked so good; it's just like he's asleep, etc.," all contribute to unrealistic shielding of the bereaved.

Much sentimentality and many a crusade are expended on the various aspects of funerals. Some do not understand that even the purchase of a casket is part of the grief work. True, many a poor widow has spent her last insurance dollar on a watertight, hermetically sealed bronze casket when she should have saved some money for the children's shoes. But this behavior needs to be viewed dynamically, not merely economically. Perhaps the best manner of dealing with this kind of unrealistic action is by preventive planning, another reason why the Church should instruct people about funerals before the crisis occurs. The too hasty critic of the lavish spender at a funeral may find himself as much of a materialist as the one whom he criticizes. Paul Tillich makes this comment about the woman who poured out the expensive ointment of pure nard upon Jesus.

What has she done? She has given an example of a waste, which, as Jesus says, is a beautiful thing. It is, so to speak, a holy waste, a waste growing out of the abundance of the heart. She represents the ecstatic

element in our relation to God, while the disciples represent the reasonable element.[16]

The problem of inordinate amounts of money being spent on flowers
falls into the same category. It needs to be re-evaluated. Roman Catholics
have been in the practice of sending "A Spiritual Bouquet." The writer
found that church people are glad for guidance in these matters. By providing a standard card for such occasions and explaining its use in advance, the members of the church were able to express sympathy and
contribute to some worthwhile cause at the same time. Simply to have
thrown out the tradition of sending flowers without providing some other
means of communicating and sharing with the bereaved would have
been arbitrary and an over-simplification of the problem.

Pastoral leadership is too often lacking when there is confusion about
policy or when the Church and its ministry is led by other more powerful
community forces. More often than not the clergy have only themselves
to blame. It is unrealistic and unfair to expect the funeral director to
know how *not* to arrange flowers in the chancel (in the case of a church
funeral) if no one was at the church to explain and interpret what can or
cannot be done in a given parish. A brief mimeographed sheet or diagram, a policy which the custodian can carry out or an authorized layman can take care of on the day of the funeral, a few words over the
phone when the arrangements are being made with the undertaker;
these and other simple devices can prevent conflict and foster good inter-
professional relationships. A minister who is personally insecure or unsure of his actual pastoral authority in matters of this kind cannot help
to formulate parish policies nor will he be able to interpret and execute
them in an effective way. He will only feel frustrated.

Some of these policy matters should be clearly understood as the
pastor's prerogative, others should be brought before the council and
congregation and be formally accepted as the procedure and policy of
the whole congregation. It does little good to become irritated with
funeral directors for their "chapel" arrangements if the laymen are un-
aware that it is not only permissible but highly expected that every
funeral (at least for members) will be from the church. The same goes
for perquisites—if abolished, the congregation should be fully informed
not to count on these "extras" as part of the pastor's salary. The matters
discussed above under "The Role of the Layman" (p. 162ff.) may also
need some minimum policy approval.

As pastor and people become convinced of the theological and psychological significance of the care of the dying, the burial and the function
of the funeral, they will give them proper study and emphasis. Ways and

---

[16] Paul Tillich, *The New Being* (New York: Scribner's Sons, 1955), pp. 46-47.

means will be found to implement appropriate policies and church practices. Confident clarification to members and community persons involved (physicians, funeral directors, florists, etc.) will minimize conflict and misunderstanding. And the Church will minister more effectively also in this great crisis of dying and in the work of grieving.

CHAPTER 12

PASTORAL CARE
AND COUNSELING

. . . shepherding is in some degree present in everything done by pastor or church. A group meeting, a sermon, or a letter may contain as much shepherding intent and effect as does a bit of personal counseling. The notion of tender and solicitous concern that is behind the metaphor is in some measure to be seen as present in everything done by pastor and church, if these are rightly done. The view of shepherding as a perspective enables us to think of shepherding as a readiness, an attitude, or a point of view that is never absent from the shepherd and is therefore in some way involved in all his feelings and actions.[1]

One of the criticisms of the state churches of Europe was that they tended to create "carriage Christians," i.e., the Church had relevance for a few highly ceremonial and festive events in life so that one rode in style to his Baptism, his confirmation, his marriage, and his burial, but that was all. We do not wish to convey the impression that the preceding five chapters, with their various sacraments, rites, or ceremonies, cover every crisis or problem in a person's life. Even when we have provided for preparation and follow-up, life simply does not come in such convenient packages or categories. In this sense pastoral care and counseling might well serve the same type of function that the term "miscellaneous" does for the accountant when he encounters expenditures that cannot be made to conform to preconceived categories of the budget. It is a way of handling the exception to the rule.

[1] Seward Hiltner, *Preface to Pastoral Theology* (New York: Abingdon Press, 1958), p. 18.

AVAILABILITY AMIDST PHYSICAL AND
MENTAL ILLNESS

What constitutes pastoral availability? Surely it takes more than ecclesiastical endorsement through ordination or the authority of the liturgy through tradition. In fact, these can be hindrances *or* helps depending upon how they are viewed and used by all concerned. It takes a pastoral attitude of concern and acceptance, of willingness to be of help when needed. The pastor must be sensitive enough to understand *what* constitutes a problem and *when* his services are needed. He will have interpreted his availability to parishioners and the community at large by the way he acts, by his use of humor (refraining from using certain types of people as butts of his jokes), by his preaching and teaching, by his statements in the press or at public gatherings. This accounts for why some church members want their hospitalization kept a secret from their minister. That minister may be formally available but not functionally.

Hospitalization is quite frequently more of a crisis than even the patient can consciously admit.[2] It is not easy to face surgery or to be told by one's physician that the diagnosis is tuberculosis involving a lengthy stay at the sanatorium. Another is told that his accident will leave him crippled for life. A childless couple need help when the young wife is told that tests have revealed her sterility. The couple needs perhaps as much help from pastoral care then as they did when they were first married; yet there is no festive ceremony for this crisis. The pastor is available for counsel and guidance at such times.

When a parishioner is committed to a mental hospital, the family often needs as much support as the patient. It is a critical break with necessary social relations and often a severe break from reality as others perceive it. While the patient is struggling with some overwhelming personal problem, society is so threatened by the symptoms that it wishes mainly to be spared the sight and so feels somewhat relieved after "sending him away." In some states there is ample "ritual," but it is mostly negative in the form of "sanity hearings" and court procedures, expert testimony, and finally, the stripping away of the simplest freedoms and civil rights, and the "verdict": *non compos mentis.*

The Church's awareness of mental illness as a crisis or struggle needing

---

[2] See the author's *Clinical Training for Pastoral Care* (Philadelphia: Westminster Press, 1956); R. D. Cabot and Russell L. Dicks, *The Art of Ministering to the Sick* (New York: The Macmillan Company, 1936); and Richard K. Young, *The Pastor's Hospital Ministry* (Nashville, Tennessee: Broadman Press, 1954); among many others dealing with pastoral care of hospital patients.

special pastoral care is of very recent origin. Anton Boisen began his pioneering chaplaincy service at Worcester State Hospital July 1, 1924.[3] By now, pastoral care of the mentally ill is becoming nearly as well-accepted among the churches as that of the physically ill. Surely pastor and laymen alike should be alert to the needs of the sick in keeping with our Lord's example and teachings.

> Then the King will say to those at his right hand, "Come, O blessed of my Father, inherit the kingdom prepared for you from the foundation of the world; . . . for I was sick and you visited me. . . ."[4]

PERSONAL AND SOCIAL PROBLEMS

> . . . I was in prison and you came to me."

Here is another experience for which there is no religious rite but rather a pervasive pastoral concern. Crime and delinquency are symbolized by the law, the courts, and an assortment of penal institutions. Everyone recognizes such behavior as social and personal failure. When the Pharisees were ready to kill the woman taken in adultery according to the law, Jesus said quietly, "You who are without sin cast the first stone." Surely the pastor has a true ministry to render when the son of one of his Deacons is thrown into jail for drunken driving. Much that was said in Chapter 10 about Holy Communion is applicable here, but there may be much personal work that must precede the more formal or sacramental type of ministry.

Divorce presupposes that personal and social problems have been festering for some time before the open break has occurred. Here too, the ceremonial part is usually legalistic, secular and negative; the church's part will be personal, evangelical, and rehabilitative. What is to take the place of the committal service in this bereavement? Who will help with the mourning, the loneliness, the sense of personal failure? This may be a much more fruitful time for therapy and guidance than a few days before the next marriage is scheduled on the rebound.

There is no ceremony for becoming a spinster. What help toward adjustment is there for the woman who faces life unmarried when she wishes so pathetically that she could have a family of her own? Can one live without enervating anxiety open to either alternative, marriage or the single state? A great many have needed help in this regard.

Housing and a vital sense of community have become a problem in

---

[3] See his *Out of the Depths* (New York: Harper and Row, Inc., 1960), Chapter 5, "An Adventure in Theological Education."

[4] *Matthew* 25:34, 36.

this age of mobility when the average family moves at least once every five years. Old rites of blessing or dedicating a dwelling have been re-studied, but are not in vogue. What of those who move into a neighbor-hood where they later discover they are a member of a minority group and subject to prejudice? Does the Church have a ministry to these social problems aside from making statements against restrictive covenants and limited occupancy? It could fall to pastoral care in part.

To whom can the person go who is denied membership in some social organization, sorority, club, etc.? Perhaps the pastor. To some these seem like little hurts that anyone should be able to brush off; but what of those for whom this is the straw that breaks the camel's back? To them it is a crisis, a reason for quitting college, changing their job, their residence.

Finally, there are those personal and social problems for which ig-norance is the cause. Not everyone is schooled in city ways, socially acceptable etiquette, minimum skills of social realtions, the elements of homemaking, etc. Here information, interpretation, and guidance are needed, not deep counseling. Wayne Oates calls this "the exploratory or short-term interview."

> Many kinds of counseling done by a pastor actually require only one conversation. He confers with a college student about a summer work opportunity. He talks with a parent about children's spending as it is related to Christian stewardship. He talks with a man and his wife about the wisdom of her changing her denomination in order to unite with the church to which her husband belongs . . . when such interviews are rightly timed, they may accomplish what dozens of therapeutic inter-views were aimed at but did not succeed in accomplishing.[5]

Vocational Issues should receive special attention. Although they are also personal and social in character, there is enough unique about them to warrant an entirely separate specialty in the counseling field: voca-tional guidance counseling. World War II highlighted the need for such guidance as several million veterans sought to find their niche again in civilian life. Vocational misplacements are often the cause of economic poverty and personal failure. Problems arise in connection with being fired, lacking motivation for one's job, and retirement. How will the Church interpret a sense of Christian vocation in future decades of in-creasing automation?[6]

Aging is not easy, nor are our people prepared for this era of life. Early

---

[5] *An Introduction to Pastoral Counseling*, edited by Wayne E. Oates (Nashville, Tennessee: Broadman Press, 1959), pp. 108-09.

[6] The author has found Donald Heiges' *The Christian's Calling* (Philadelphia: Muhlenberg Press, 1959) helpful in instances of vocational guidance. It shows the religious dimensions of daily work in a realistic way.

retirement and lengthening years due to medical advancements have made this as definite a period to be dealt with as the transition from childhood to adulthood. Will the Church develop something similar to the adolescents' confirmation or is "visiting the shut-ins" enough? Here is an open field for research and pioneering to expand the Church's ministry in a very real problem area.

THE CHURCH AS A RESOURCE

In small congregations people become aware of each other's need on an informal basis by word of mouth. They will call up on the phone or stop over for a visit much as members of a large family. With close personal acquaintance there comes an intuitive sense of when and how to help one another. It is not unusual to see a little cluster of old friends check up on one of their number who is shut-in or troubled and keep each other informed about his or her welfare. There is no need to call in a group of highly trained professionals to "handle the case" if members of the primary friendship group have everything under control.

The author recalls a seventy-eight year old shut-in who had not been out of her apartment for a dozen years. He brought Communion once a month and made a pastoral call between times so that he was in touch with her about twice a month. It was very seldom that some one else from the church had not just been there or was not going to come in a day or so. And this kept up without any committee assignment or other mechanics for year after year.

Larger churches need more organizational structure because the members attending multiple services of worship and living far from one another may not even be aware of each other's needs. We want to help everyone take as much active part in the life and fellowship of the Church as possible. All need to discover that the Church is willing and able to serve, to meet the needs of each individual that he may find the abundant life.

Churches actively concerned about the whole man and desirous of utilizing their whole potential and resources will have members that resemble the Good Samaritan of Jesus' parable rather than the "carriage Christians" referred to at the beginning of this chapter.

REFERRAL FOR OTHER HELP [7]

In spite of what has been said about the wonderful resources of Christian love and fellowship in the church, there comes a

---

[7] *See Where To Go For Help* by Wayne E. Oates (Philadelphia: Westminster Press, 1957), for a thorough discussion of the "helping professions," thirteen typical

time when the problem is so deep or complex that only the professionally trained person is "good enough." We see this quite obviously in the case of cancer, psychosis, or the fitting of contact lenses. It is a bit harder to discriminate in the borderland areas. The writer can only testify that he has usually been glad when he played it safe instead of trying to bluff his way in waters that were over his head. He was glad he had referred a distraught service man who had been given a hardship discharge because of the illness of his wife and young child, for psychiatric consultation. Meanwhile, he continued to make pastoral calls and do what marriage counseling he thought useful. But through suggestions over the course of many months, the man voluntarily submitted to a ten-day stay in the local mental hospital for diagnosis, testing, and interviews. Four months later, when the man murdered his wife with a hammer, the pastor was glad he had not "carried the case alone." At least all the knowledge, skills, and best trained judgments in the community had been used.

The church need not apologize for referring to "secular" resources. A proper understanding of the doctrines of creation and providence and the perspective of "natural revelation" should make it possible for the pastor to view the so-called secular disciplines of science, medicine, law, psychology, social work, education, etc., as also under the domain of God's universe and thus partners with the Church Universal. What is more, Christian laymen are to be found in all these fields fulfilling their Christian vocations. In a sense the Church is there too, for these believers do not leave the Church while they go about their various tasks.

Naturally, care must be taken to refer only when it is appropriate. The minister who refers every little worry or disappointment to a psychiatrist will lose the respect of others. But it is doubtful if that is the stance of most clergy. Rather they are too reticent. It has been the writer's experience that when he has approached one of the other professions for referral help, they have rolled out the red carpet of hospitality, have given generously of their time, and were genuinely pleased that the Church was expressing this willingness to cooperate for the good of some individual in need. Here the Church is seen at its best, not as a vested interest fighting over the territorial rights of some person's soul in a denominational tug of war. Here the Church is willing to minister rather than to be ministered unto.

What is the relation between all this discussion of pastoral care, counseling, social problems, referral, and the various sacraments and rites dis-

problem areas for which specialized help is often needed, and a directory of agencies with addresses on the national and local levels.

Local welfare councils, community chest, or united fund offices willingly distribute current directories of health and welfare services. County welfare boards and state departments of public welfare also provide lists of services and agencies.

cussed in previous chapters? It is true that some of these problems not only fall between the formal provisions of these ceremonies, but very often these problems make the formal ministrations of the Church unavailable to the individual so suffering. For example, a person who believes she is the Virgin Mary, cannot benefit from Holy Communion. The person who is so filled with shame and remorse that he isolates himself from society may also separate himself from the worshipping community of the Church. He is not even exposed to the preaching of the Word of God and the reconciliation of the Gospel. Seeing our neighbor in need automatically becomes a command of love from the Good Shepherd to care for him with all the resources at our disposal.

CONCLUSION

We return to the function of practical theology. "Practical theology consists of those principles and methods needed to make the Gospel applicable to society and meaningful to the individual." It was also suggested that a foundation was needed in the systematic, biblical, and historical branches of theology in order to do this. One needs to do the right thing for the right reason. In our generation of activism and superficial standards of "success," we are already too prone to act on the basis of utilitarian expediency.

When we speak about meeting the needs of individuals amidst the great issues of their lives, we can not mean a simple hedonistic lack of discomfort and be true to the full teachings of Christ. What of the martyr, the prophet, the Suffering Servant? We can pay too high a price for "peace of mind"—perhaps the Scribes and Pharisees of Jesus' day did. In fact, a misunderstanding of this very point has provided many a superficial preacher with a vulnerable straw man to knock down in his sermon.

Creeds and doctrines provide much needed perspective as checks and balances upon our work in the Church. They are by no means as dull and static as some think. They are the condensed consensus of thousands of years of biblical and churchly experience. Many a fad and heresy has come and gone because it did not measure up to the central and essential concerns of the Christian message. Thus the creeds serve as chart and the Word of God serves as compass for the troubled seas of each generation. And the Church's mission is to keep the passengers safe against the storm of life.

We have nòt pretended to discuss all the aspects of practical theology. There are many other functions of the Church and appropriate methods, skills, and theories that need to be discussed. There are the matters of evangelism and Christian education, which have only been touched on tangentially. Homiletics and church administration, missions at home and abroad, stewardship, ethics, and so forth, all need to receive attention commensurate with their great importance in the life of the Church.

Our thesis has been to show the dynamic significance of the great liturgies of the Church for the life of the individual. If the treatment has appeared in places to be apologetic in character, it is because the author has derived personal help in so viewing the ministry of the Church. He believes firmly that faith is a gift of God, but to see it in action is always a blessed and reassuring experience. He has seen the healing and empowering grace of God through Christ brought to people in the ministry of the Church to the crises of life.

INDEX

260
B42

DATE DUE